Mandala Coloring Book

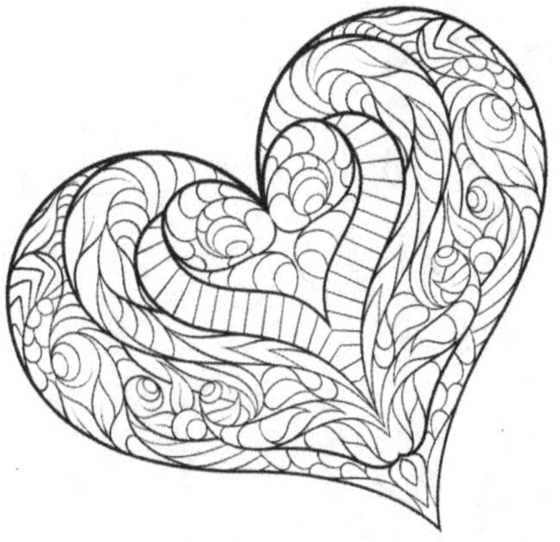

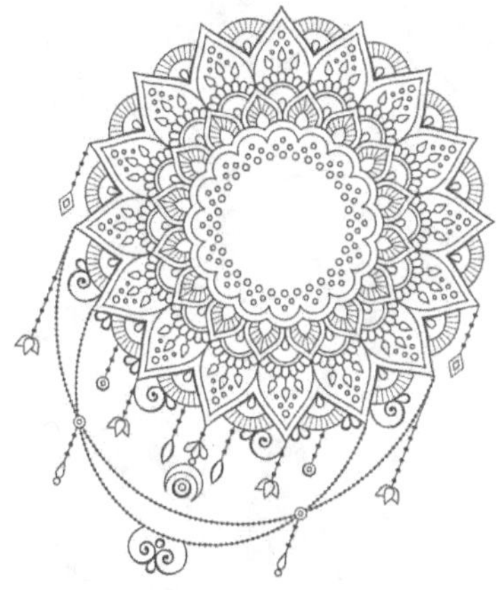

This book belongs to :

....

....

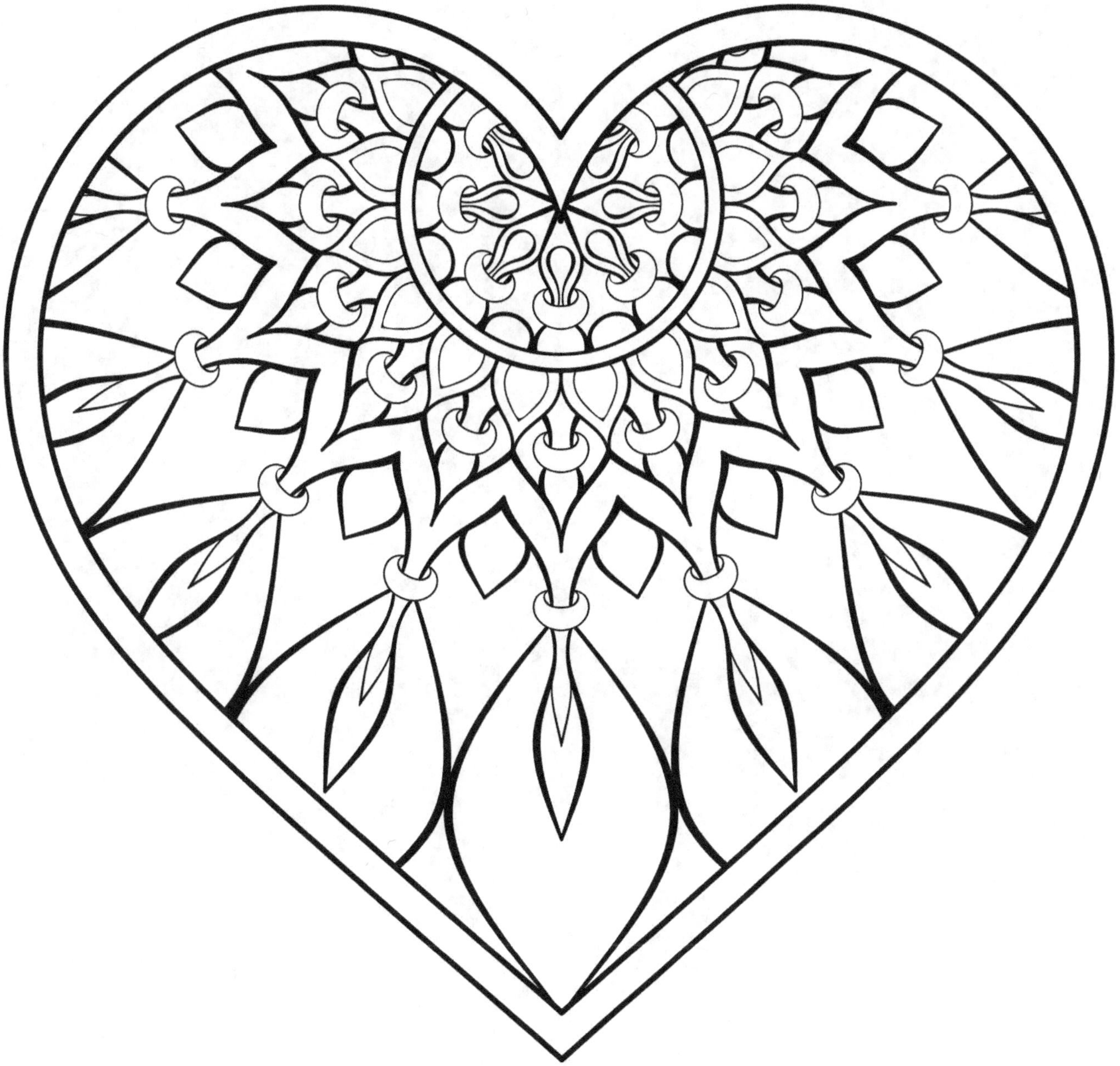

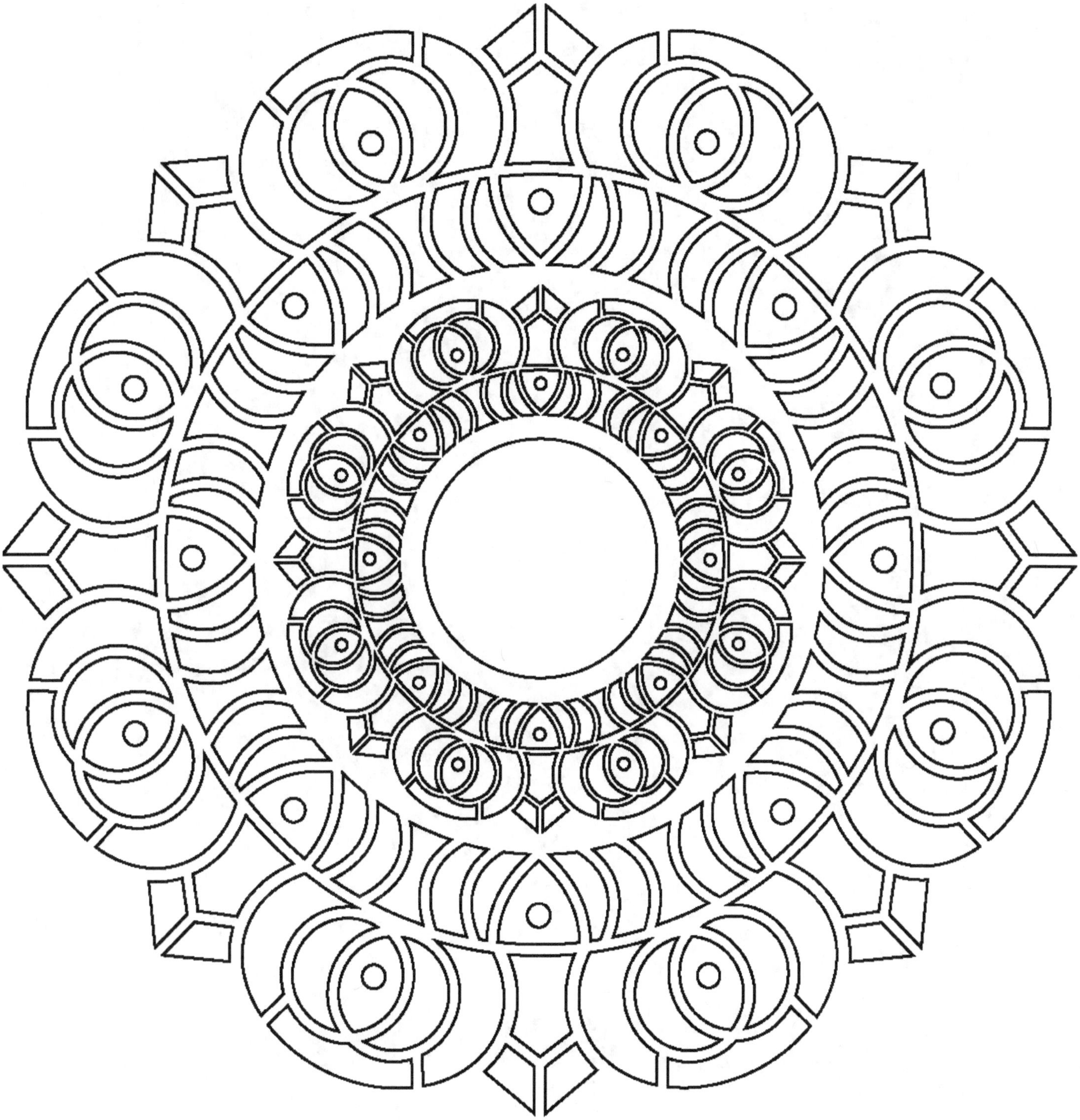

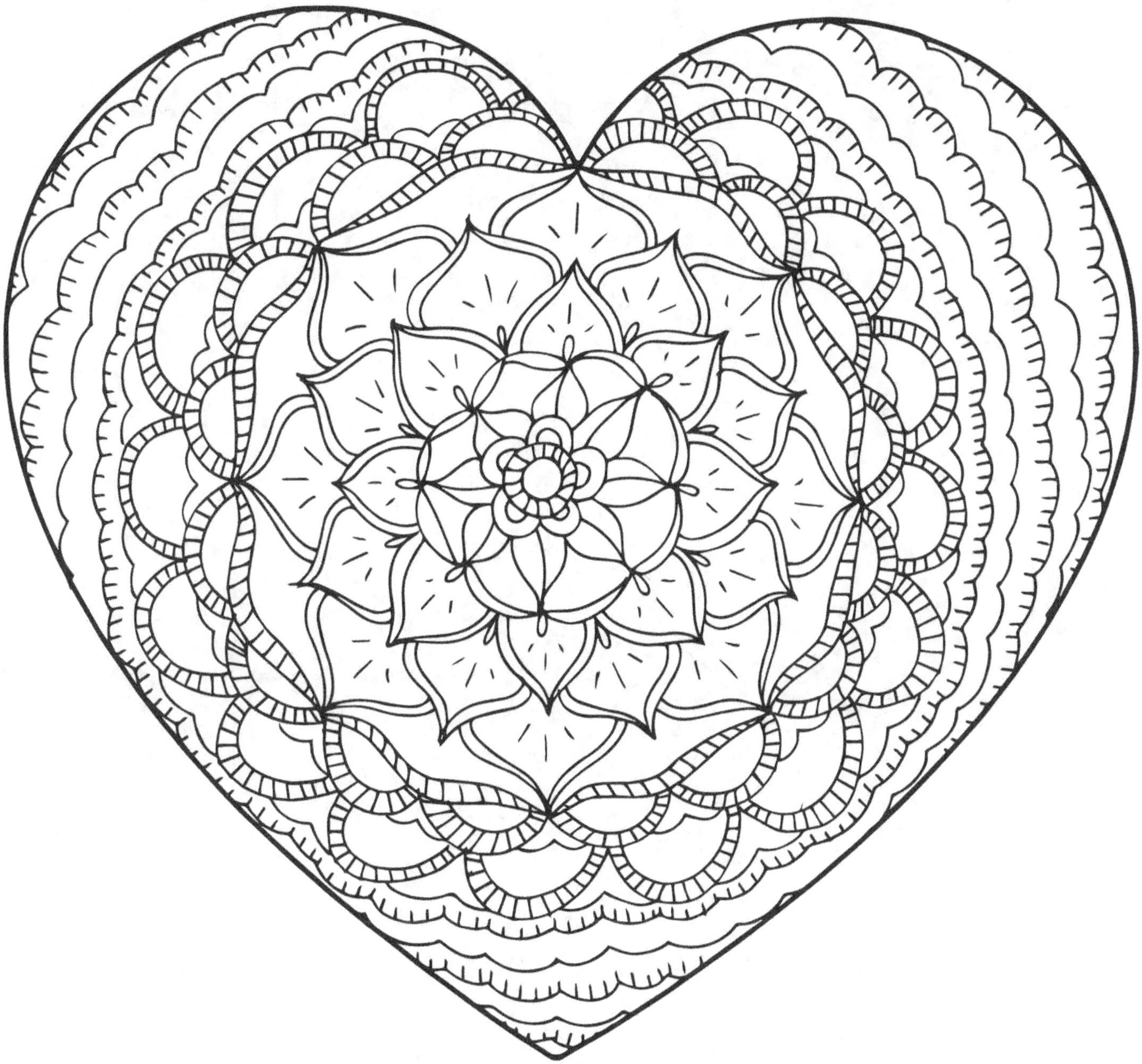

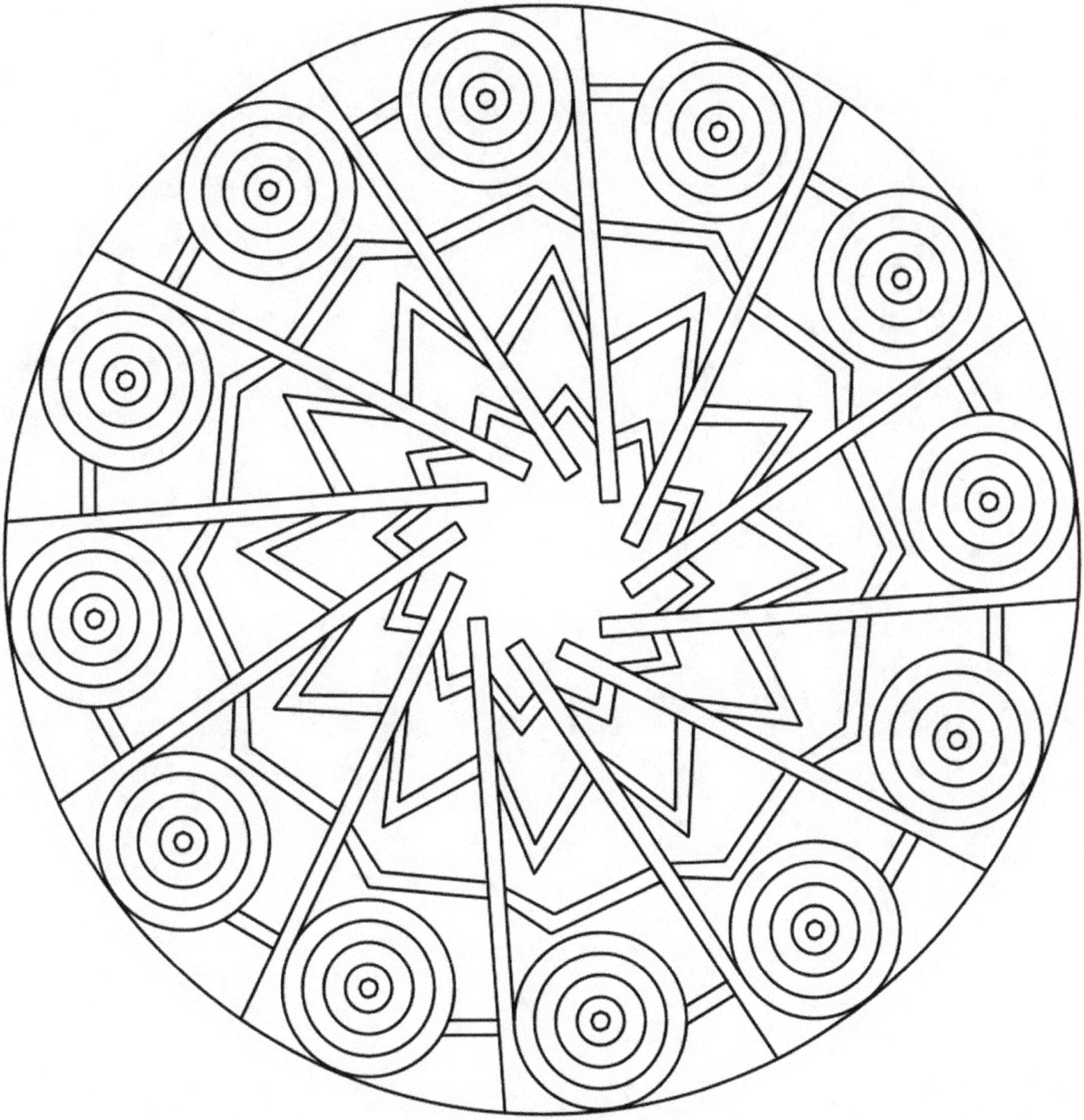

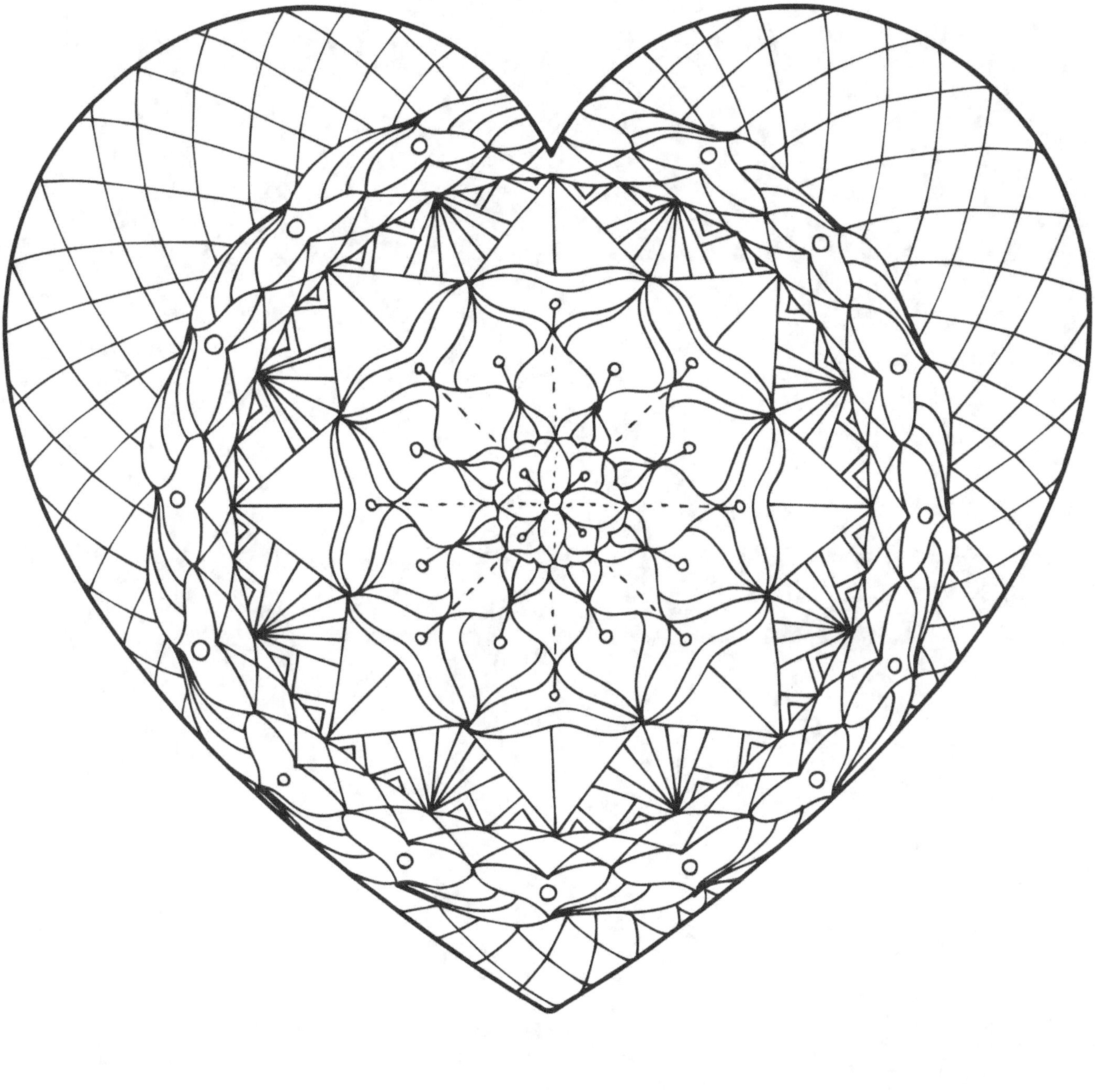

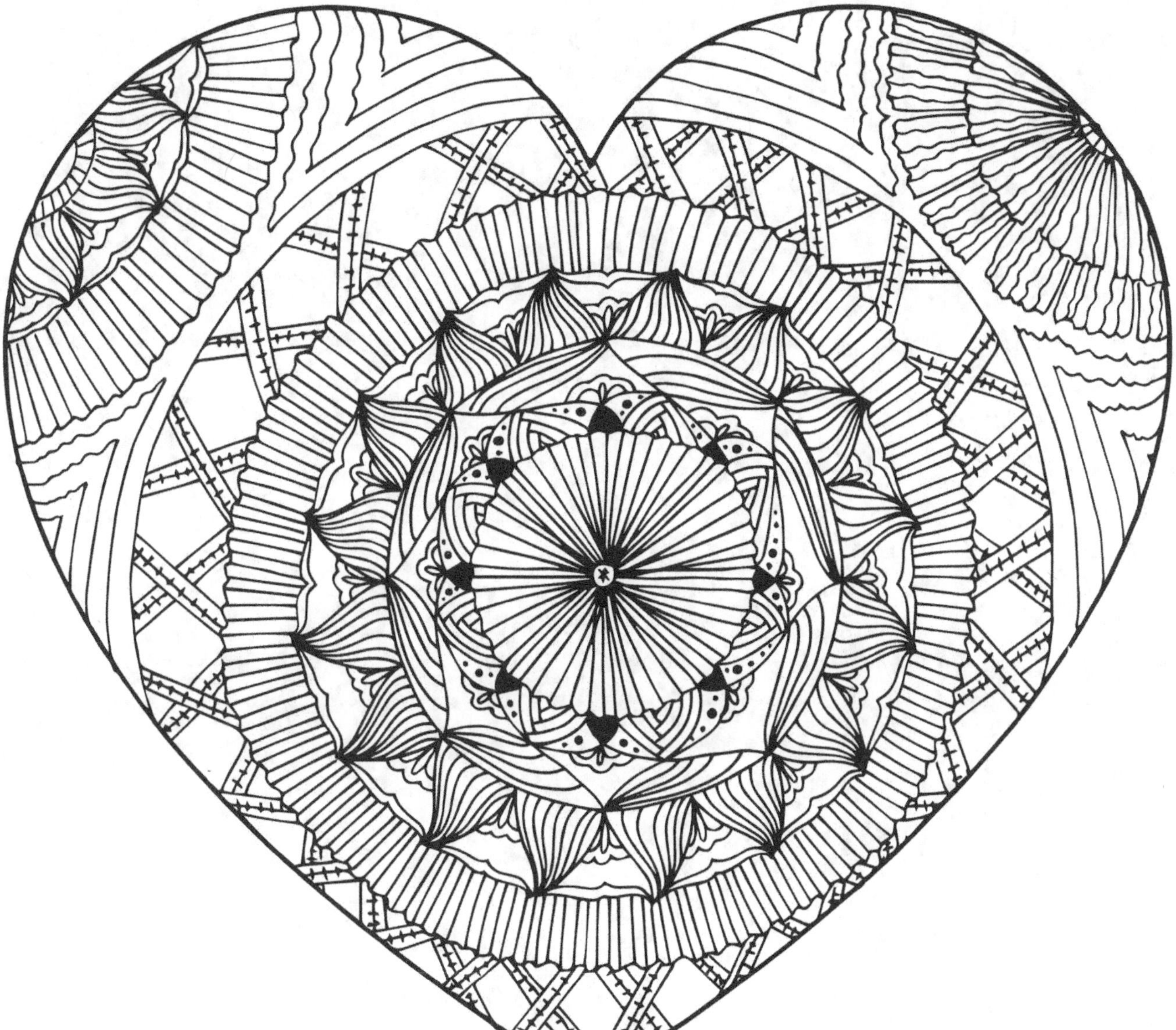

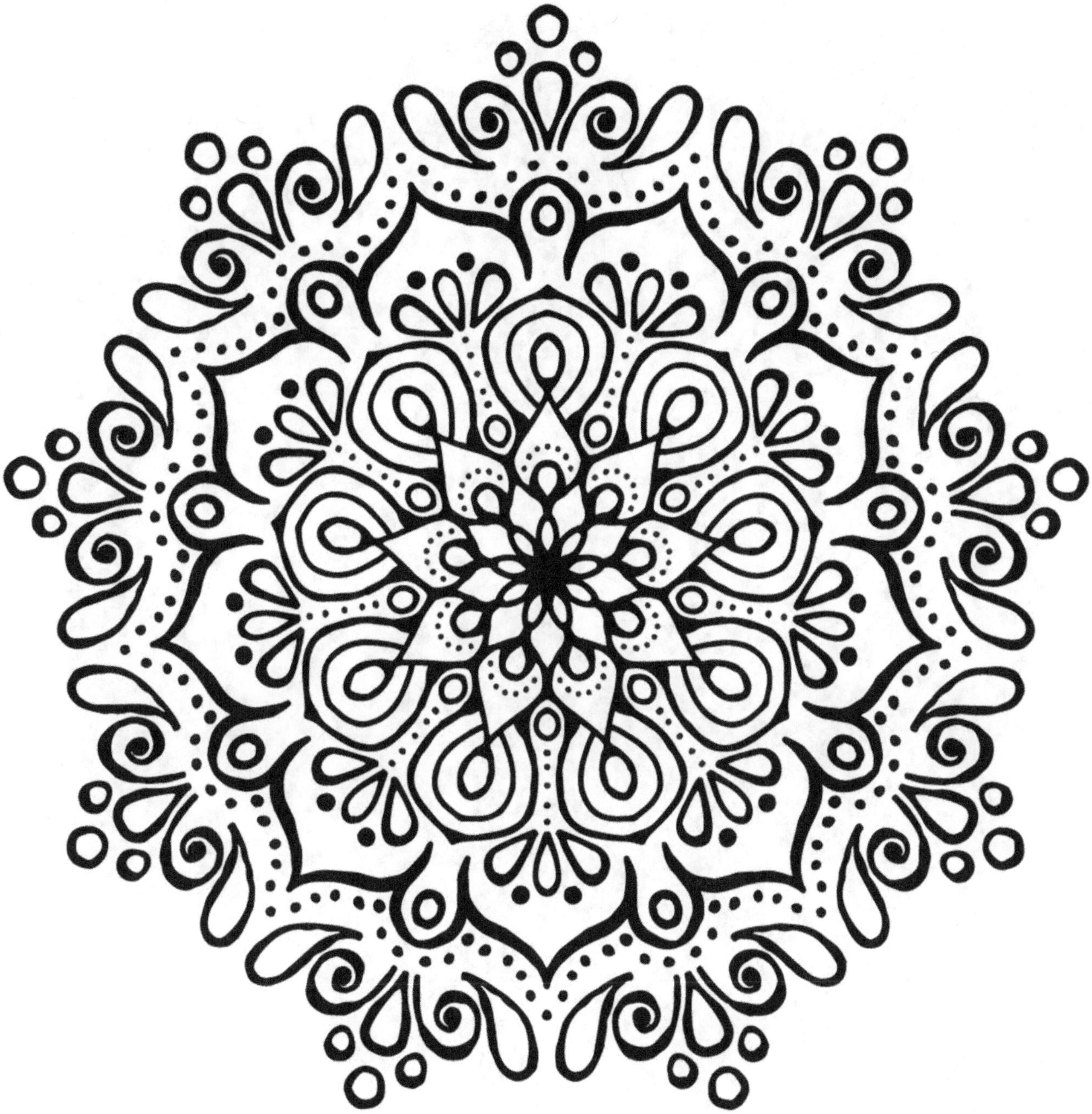

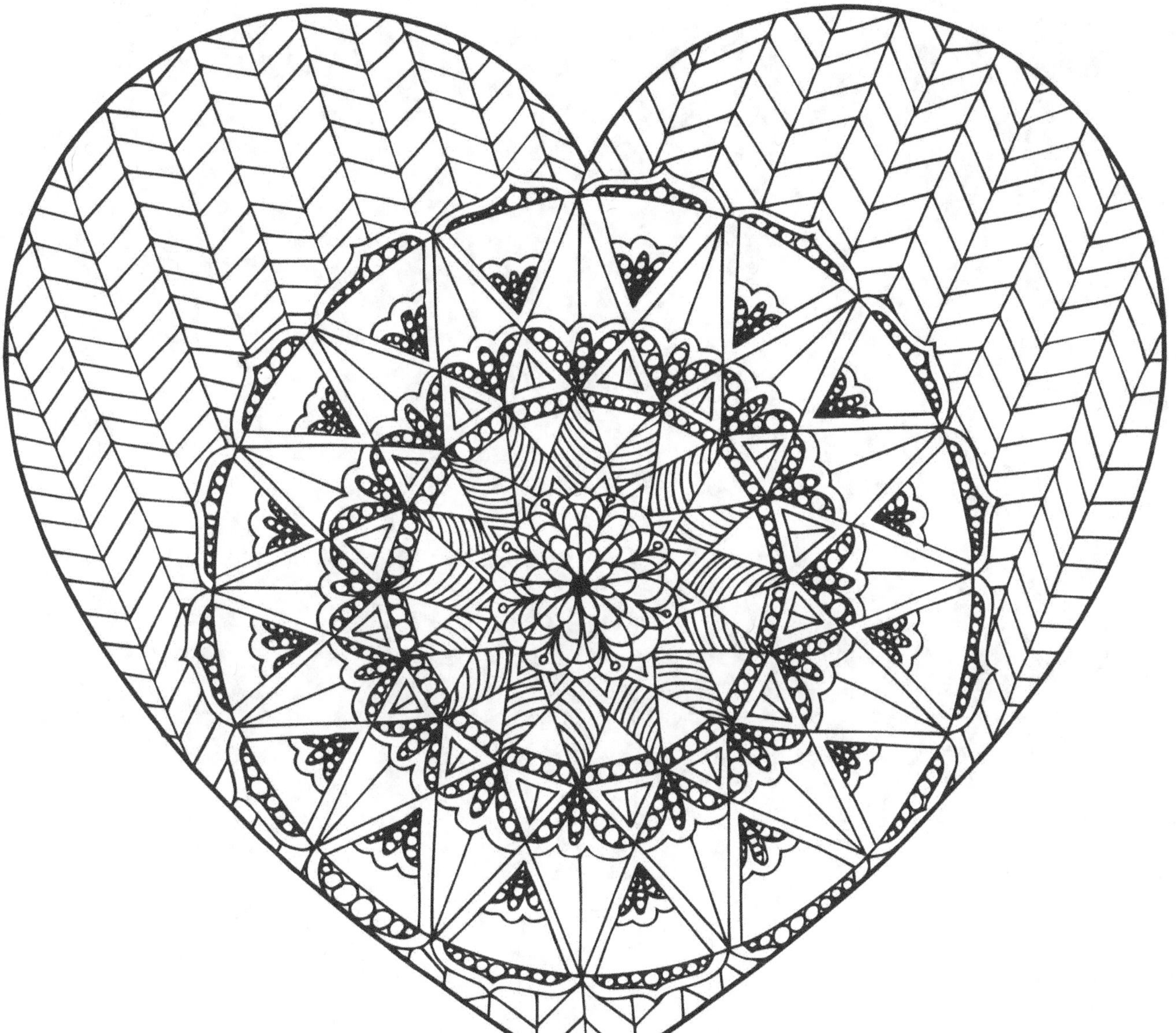

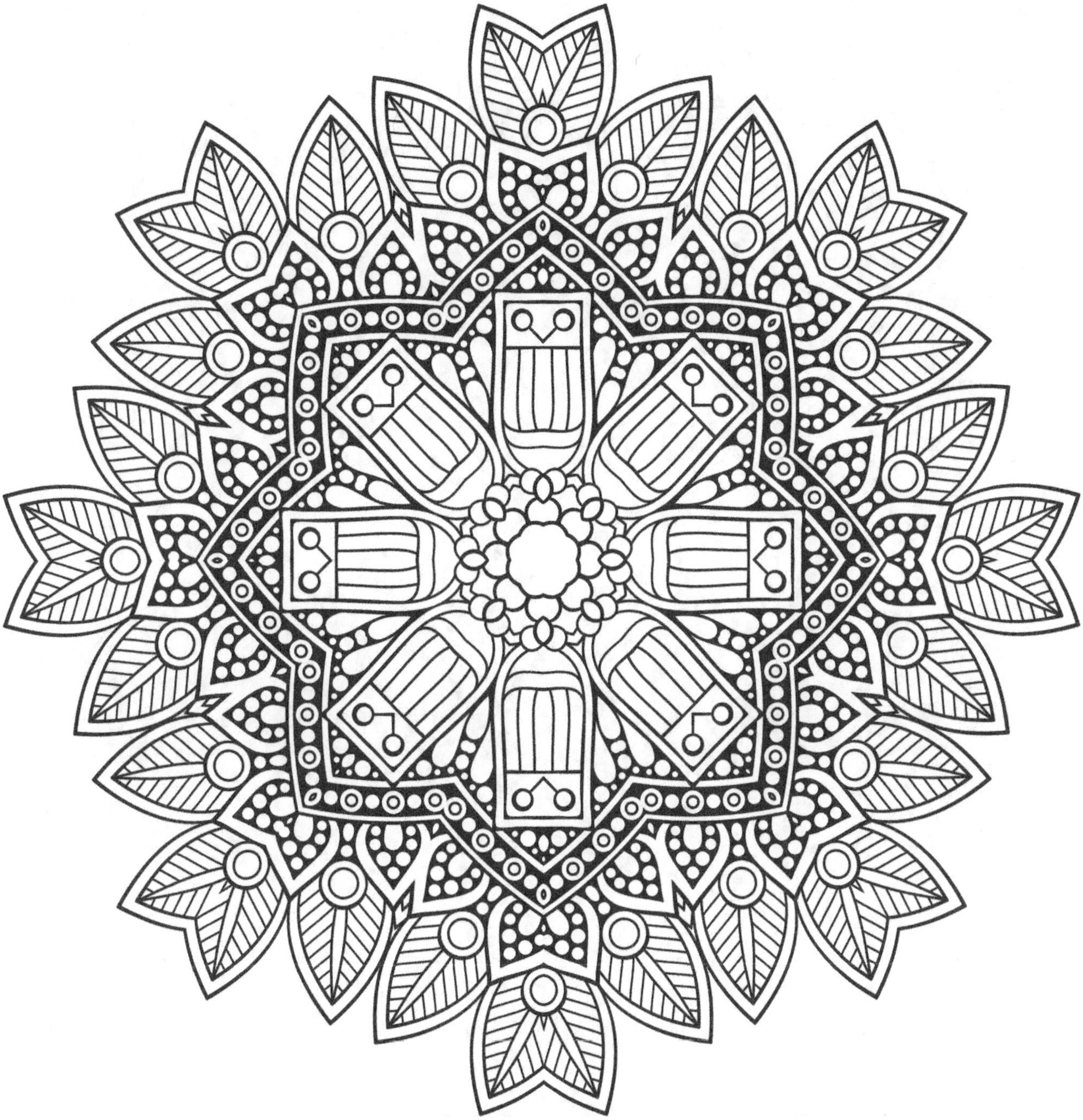

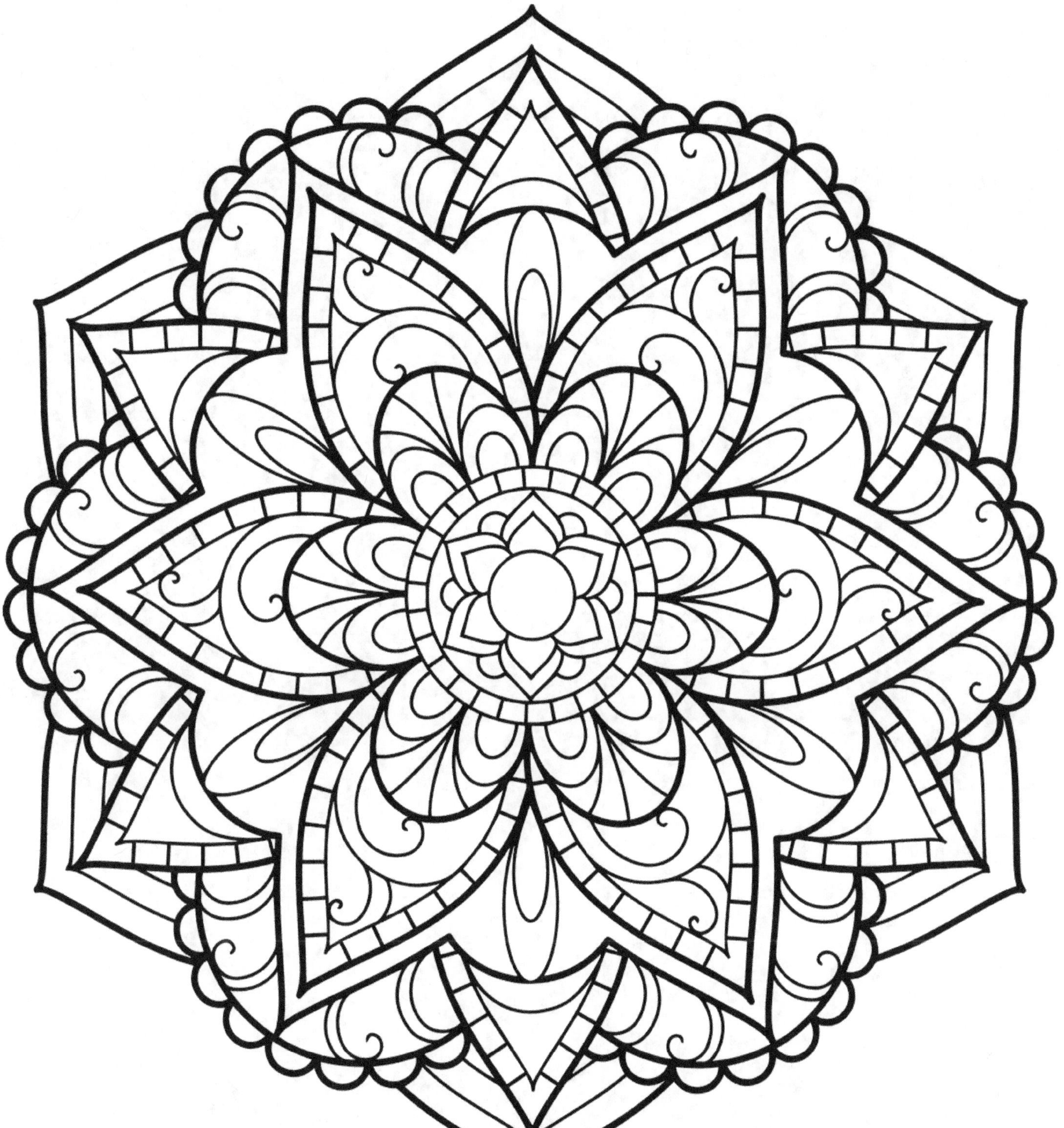

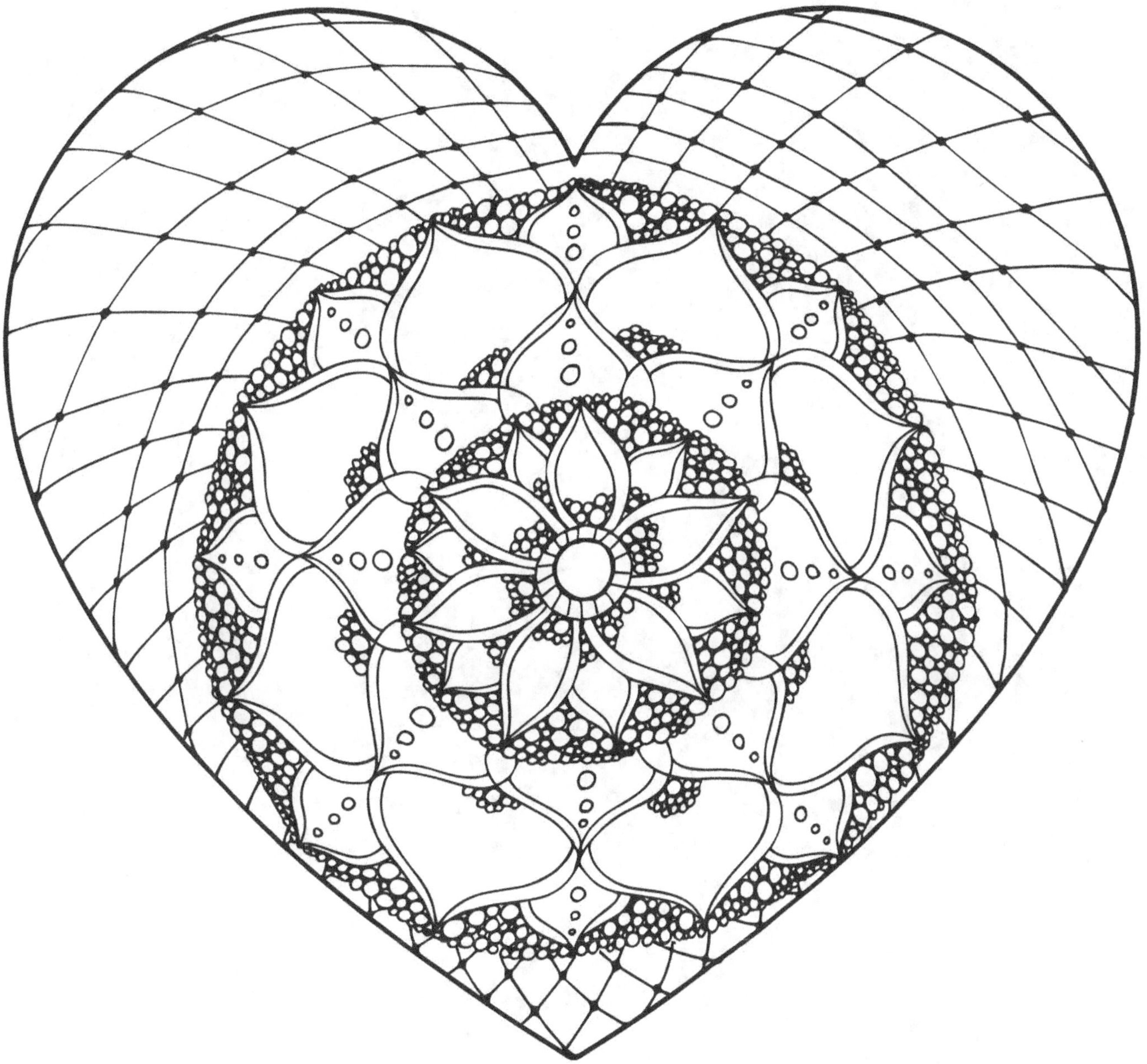

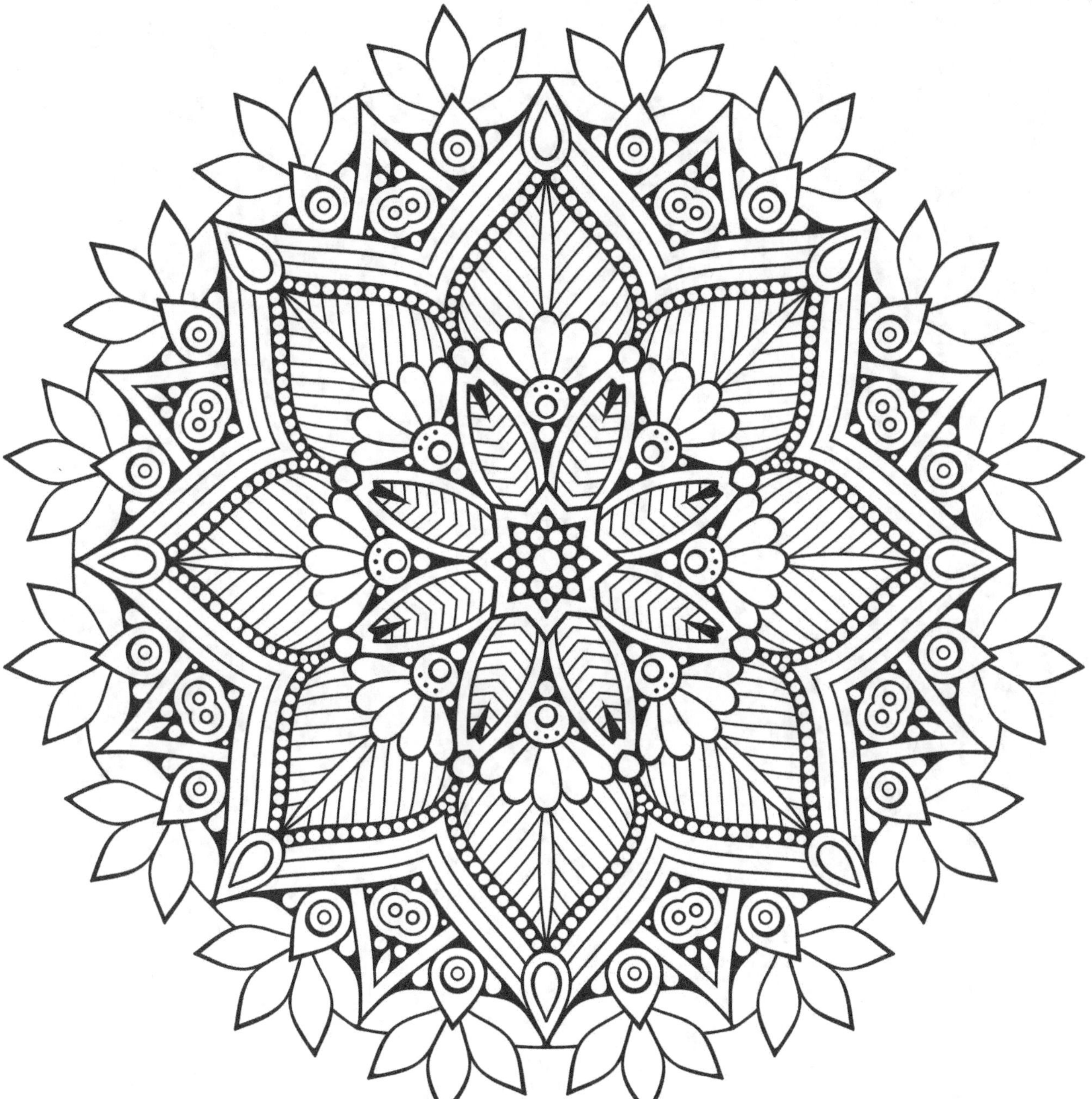

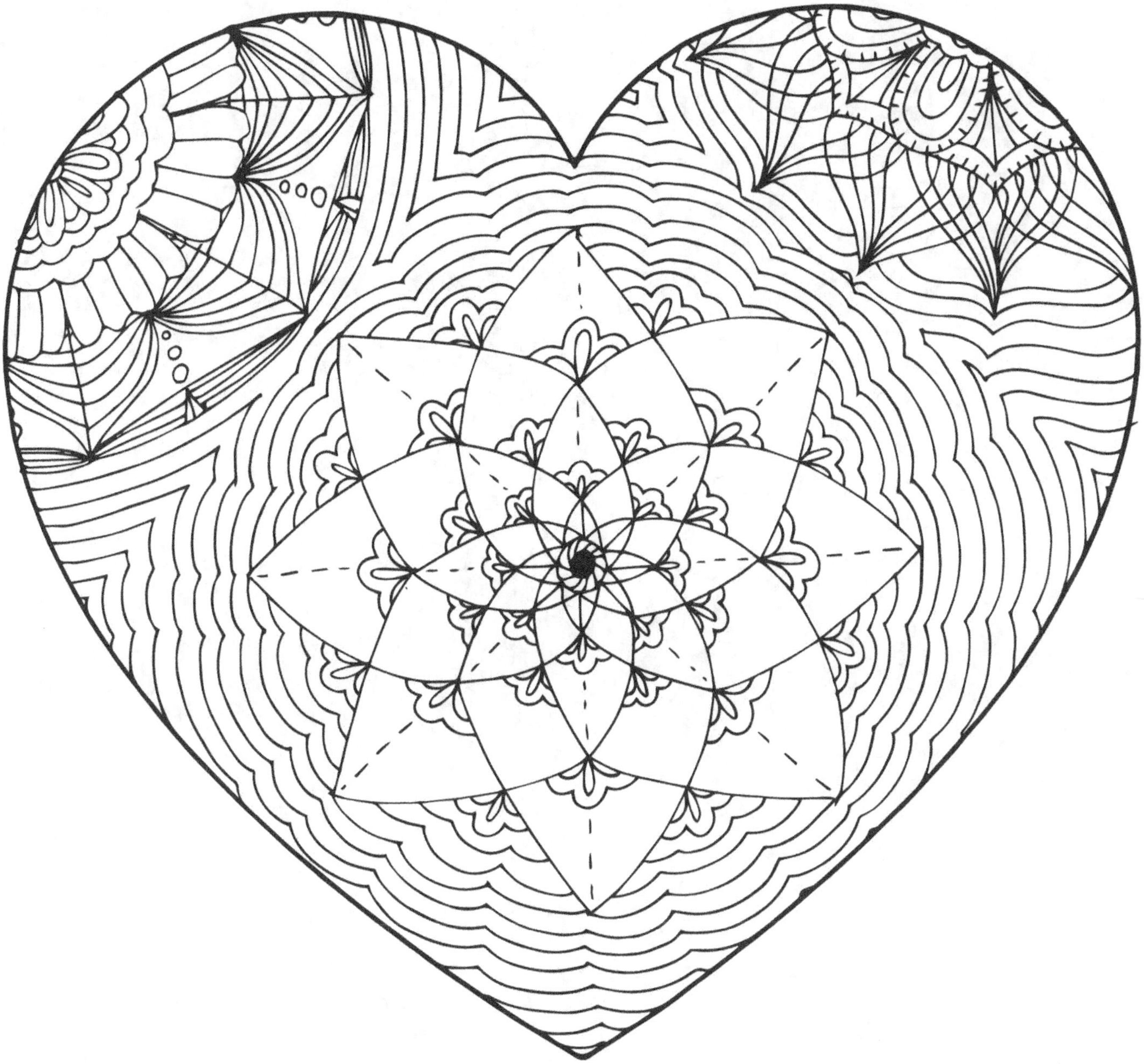

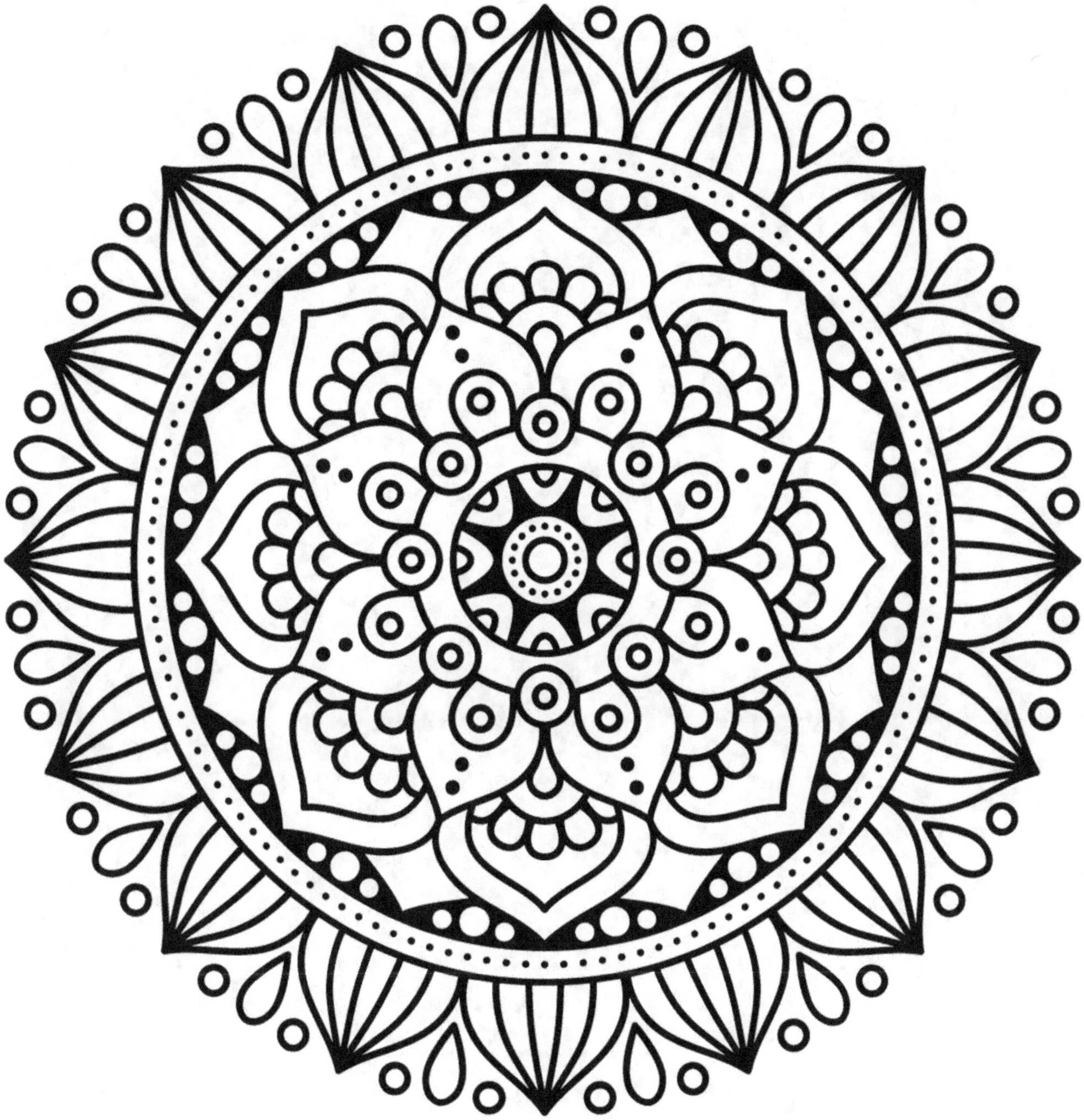

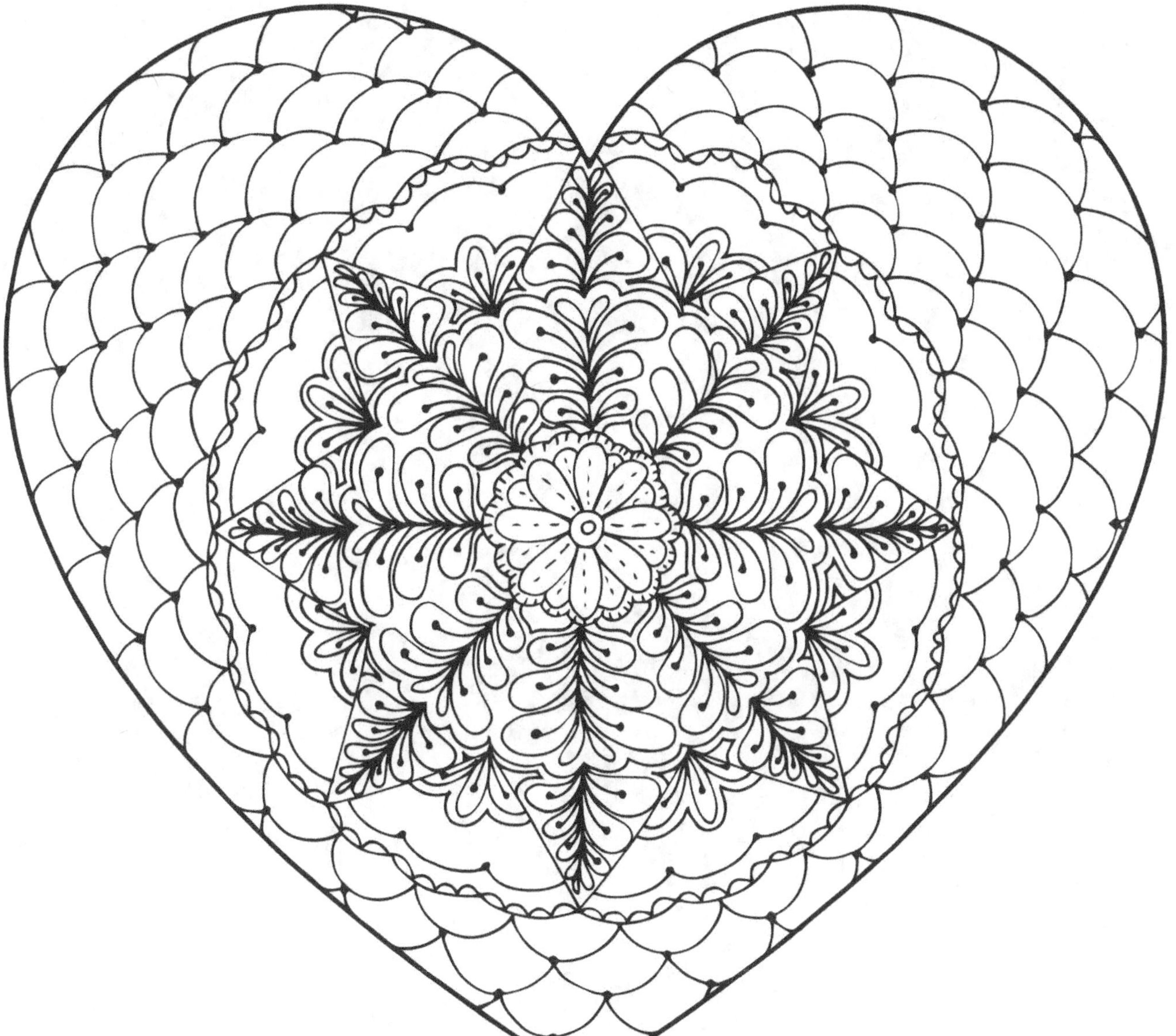

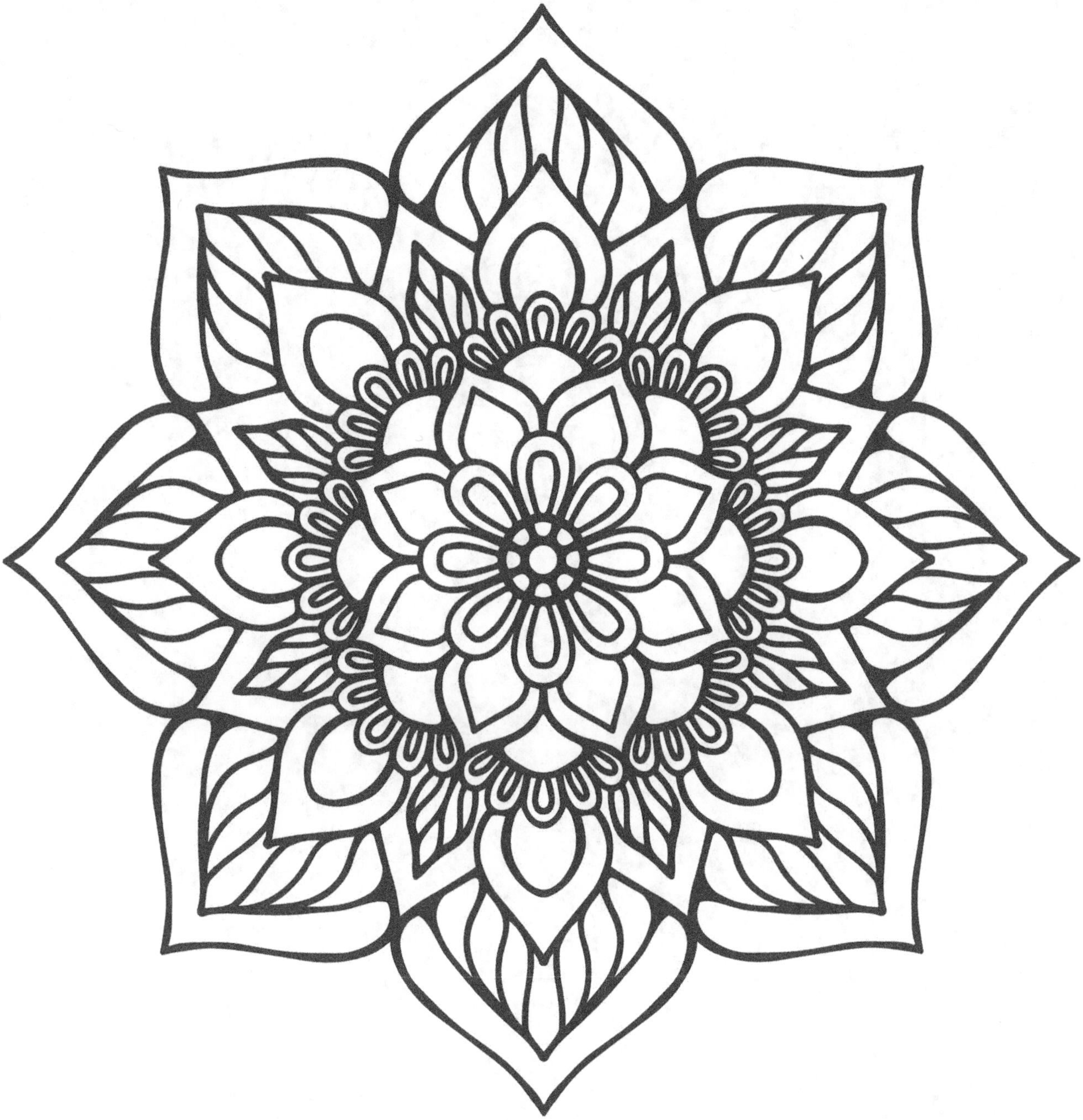

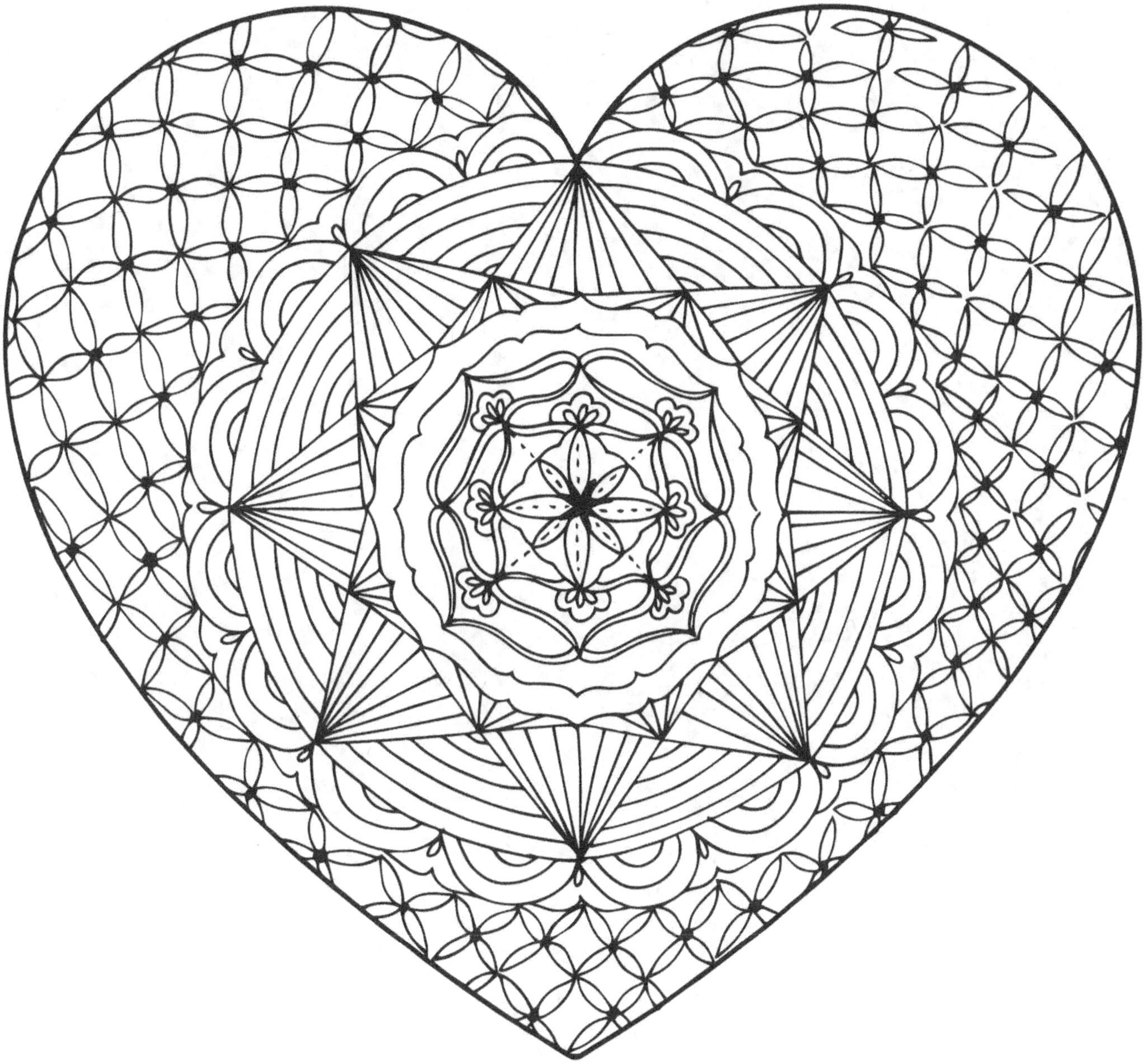

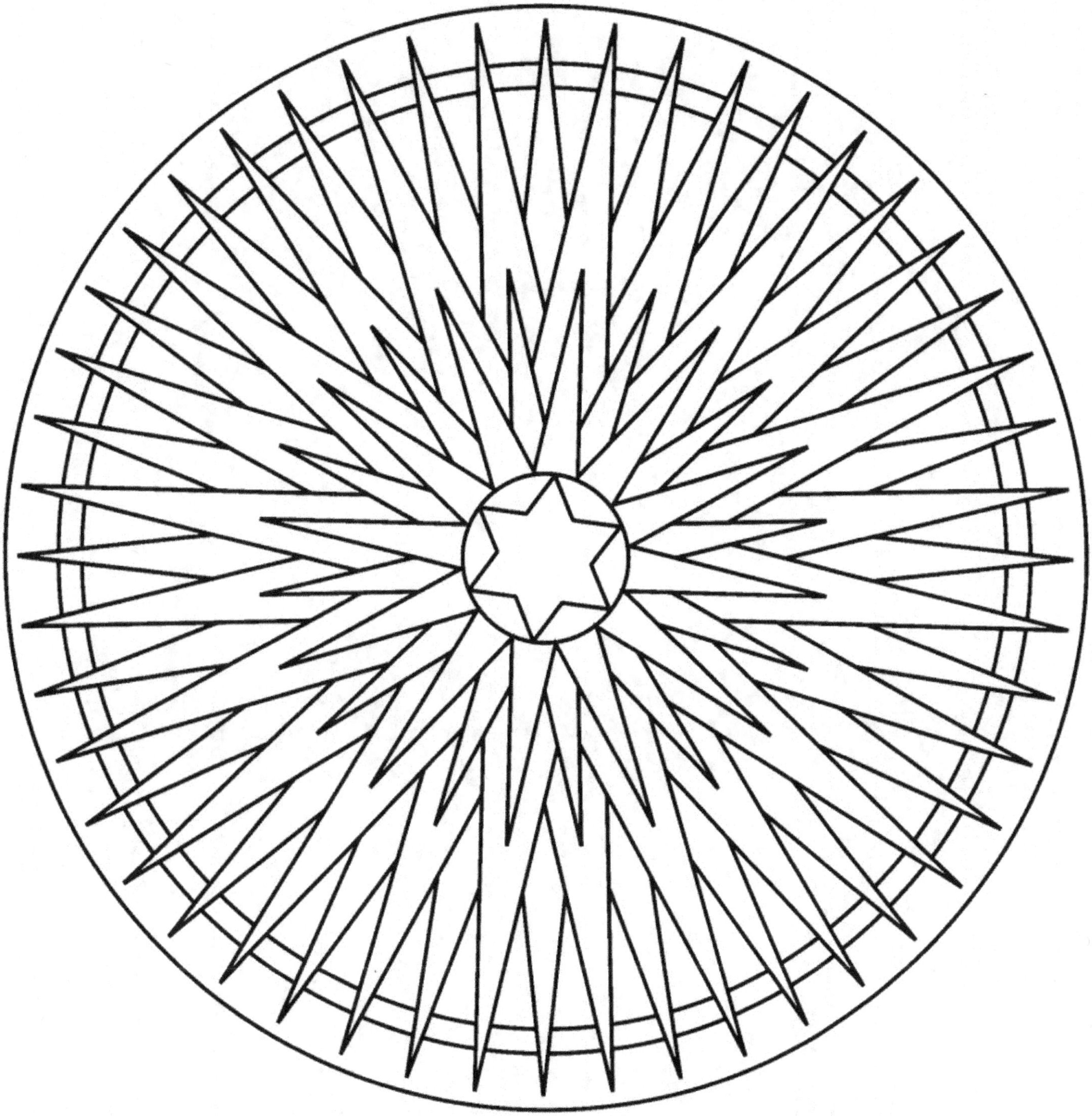

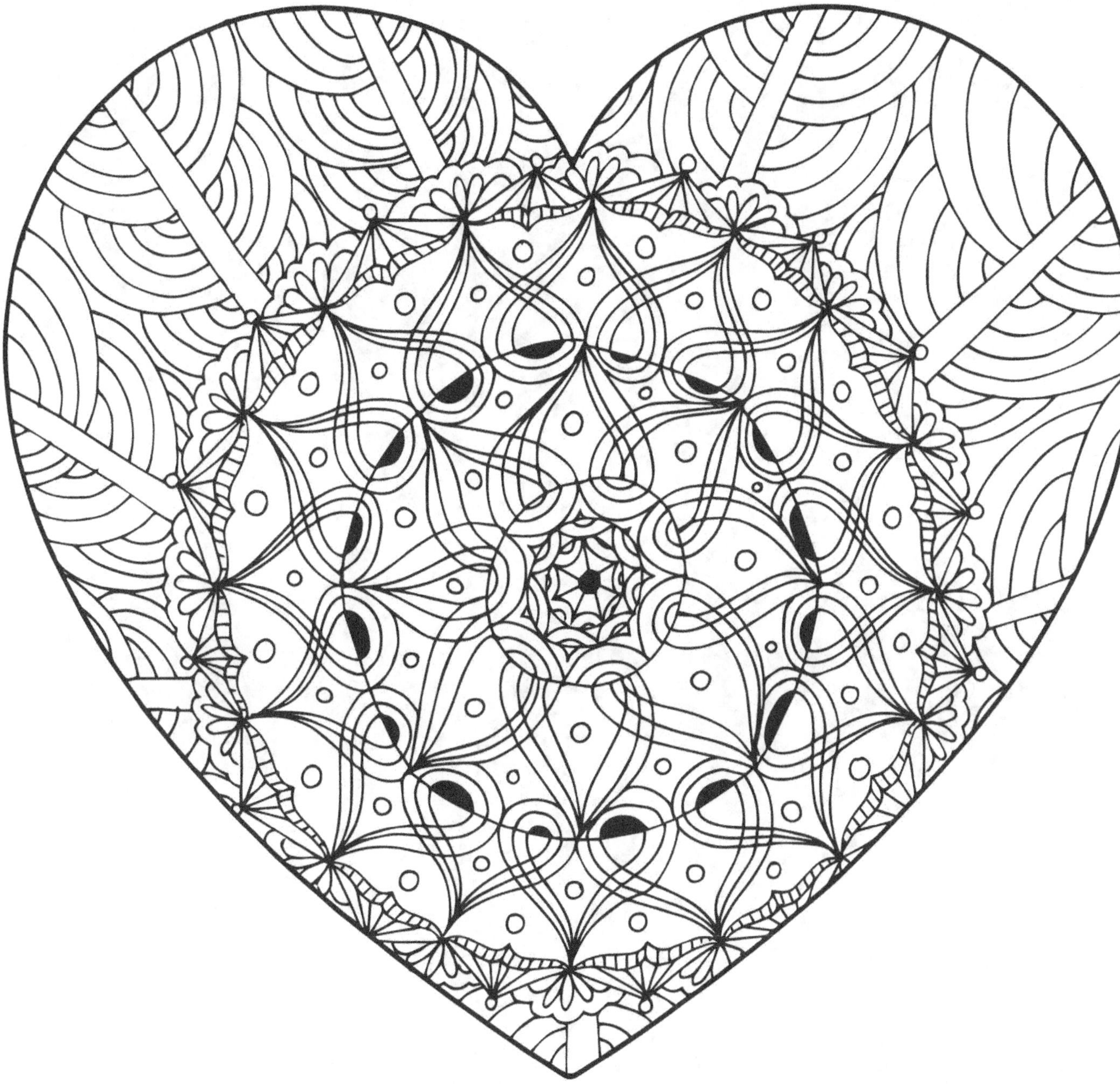

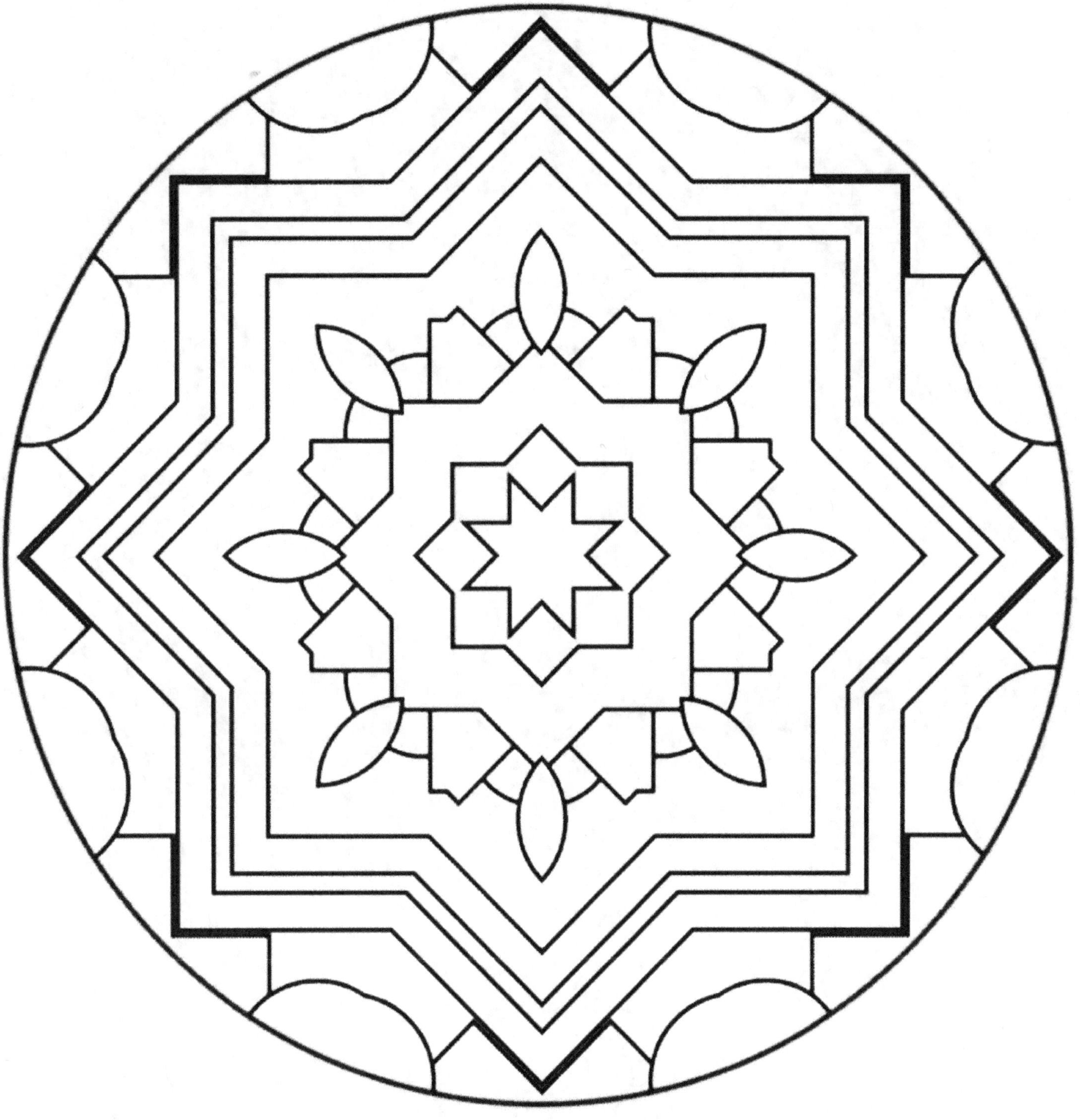

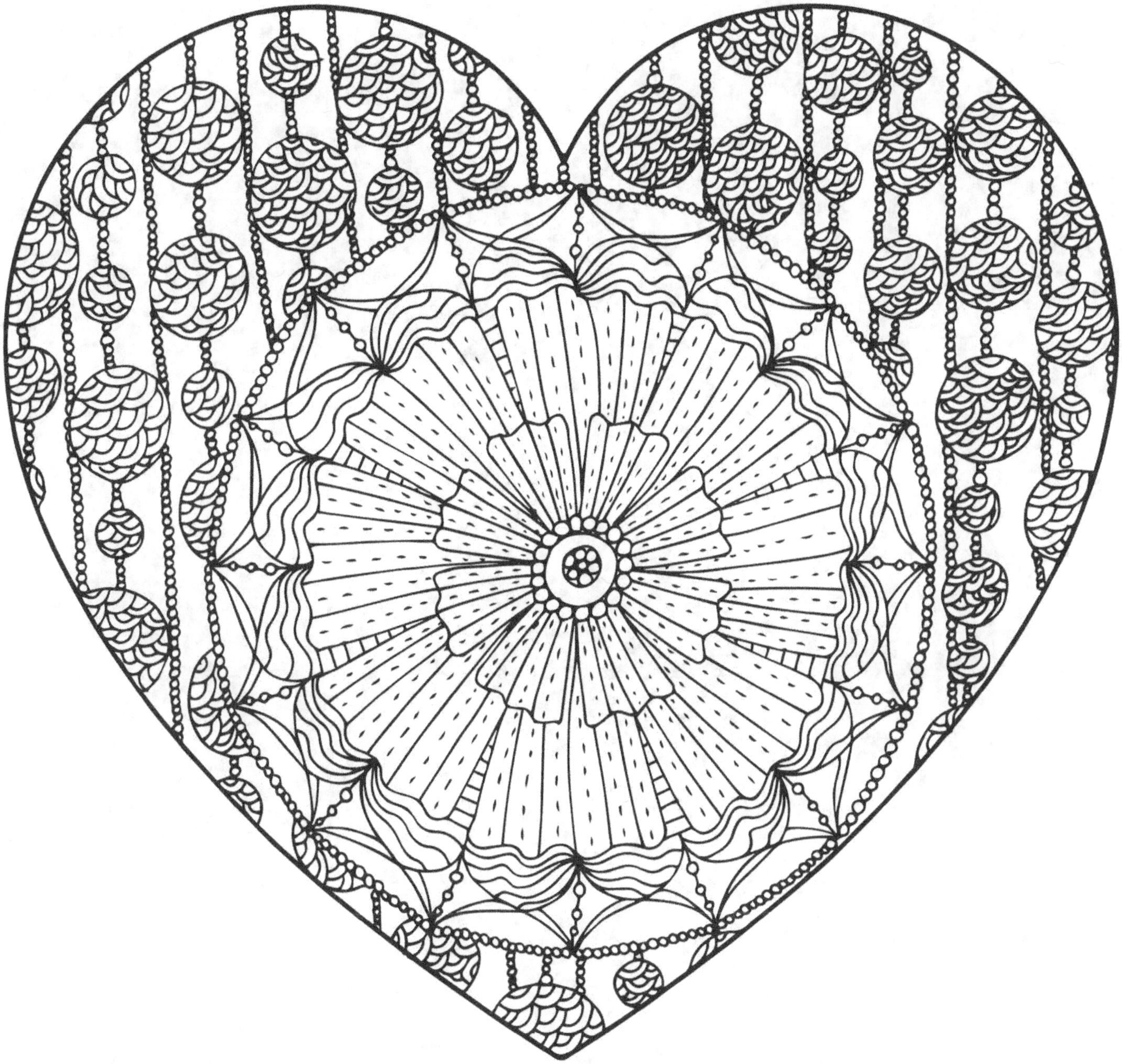

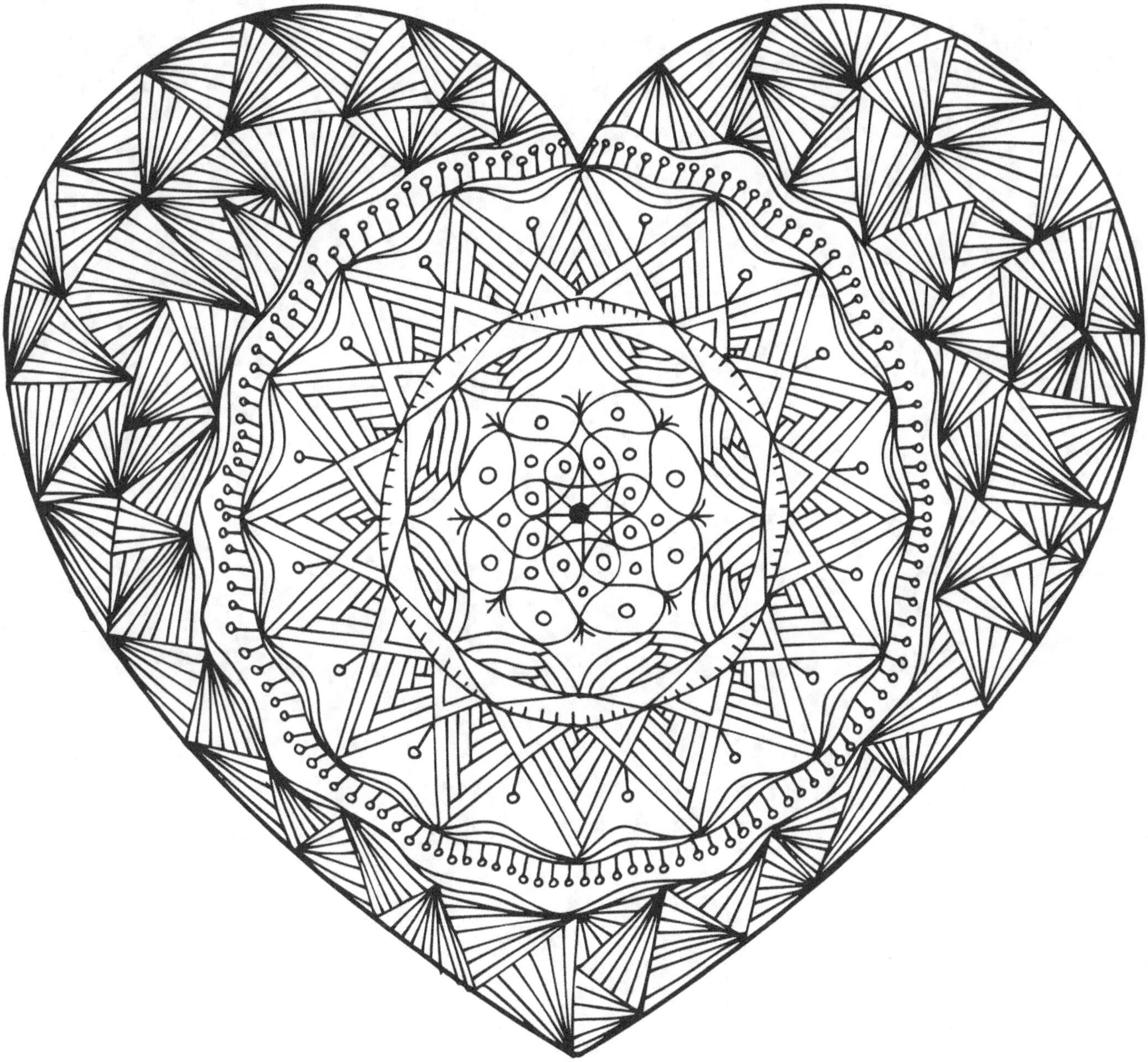

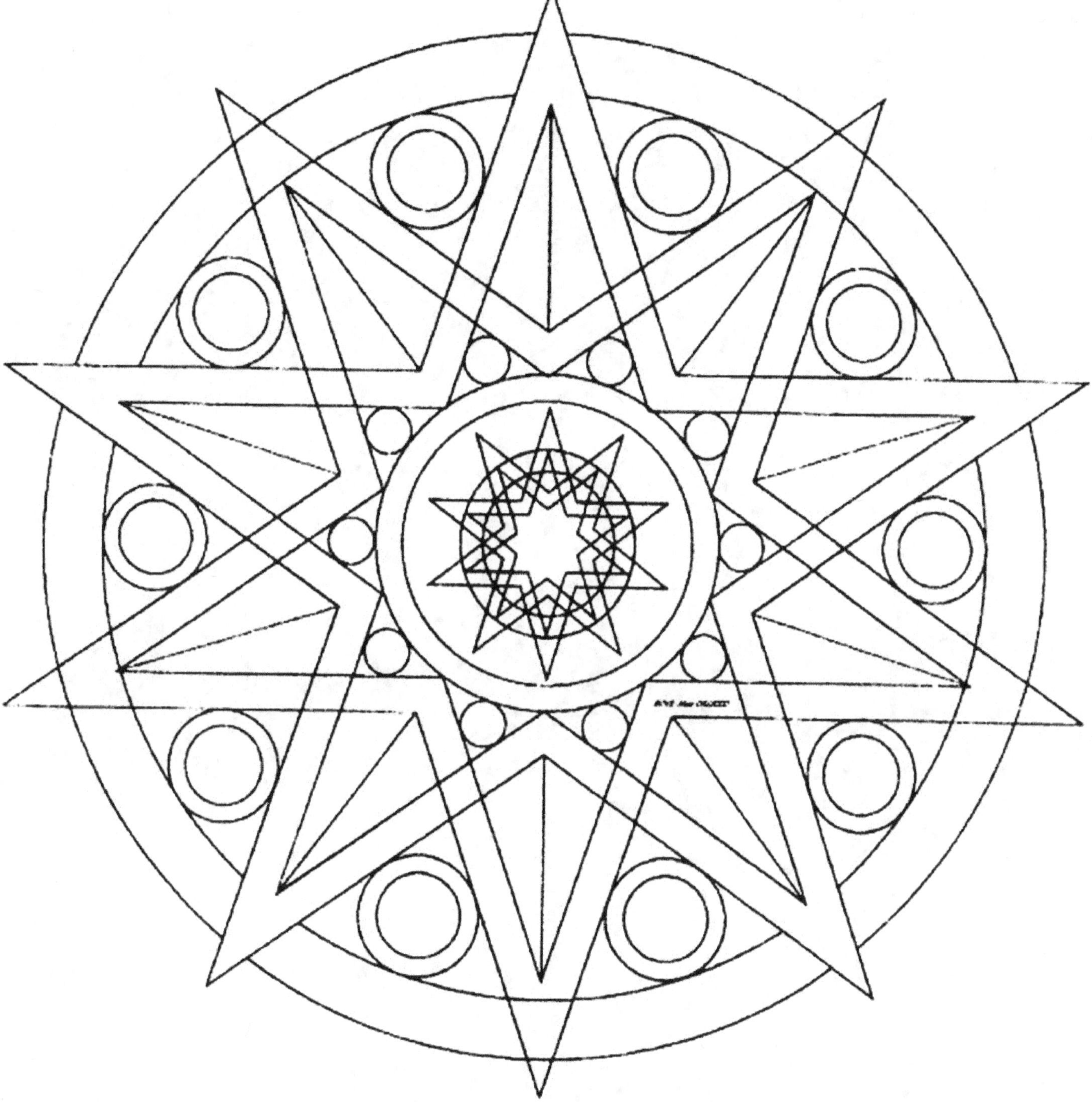

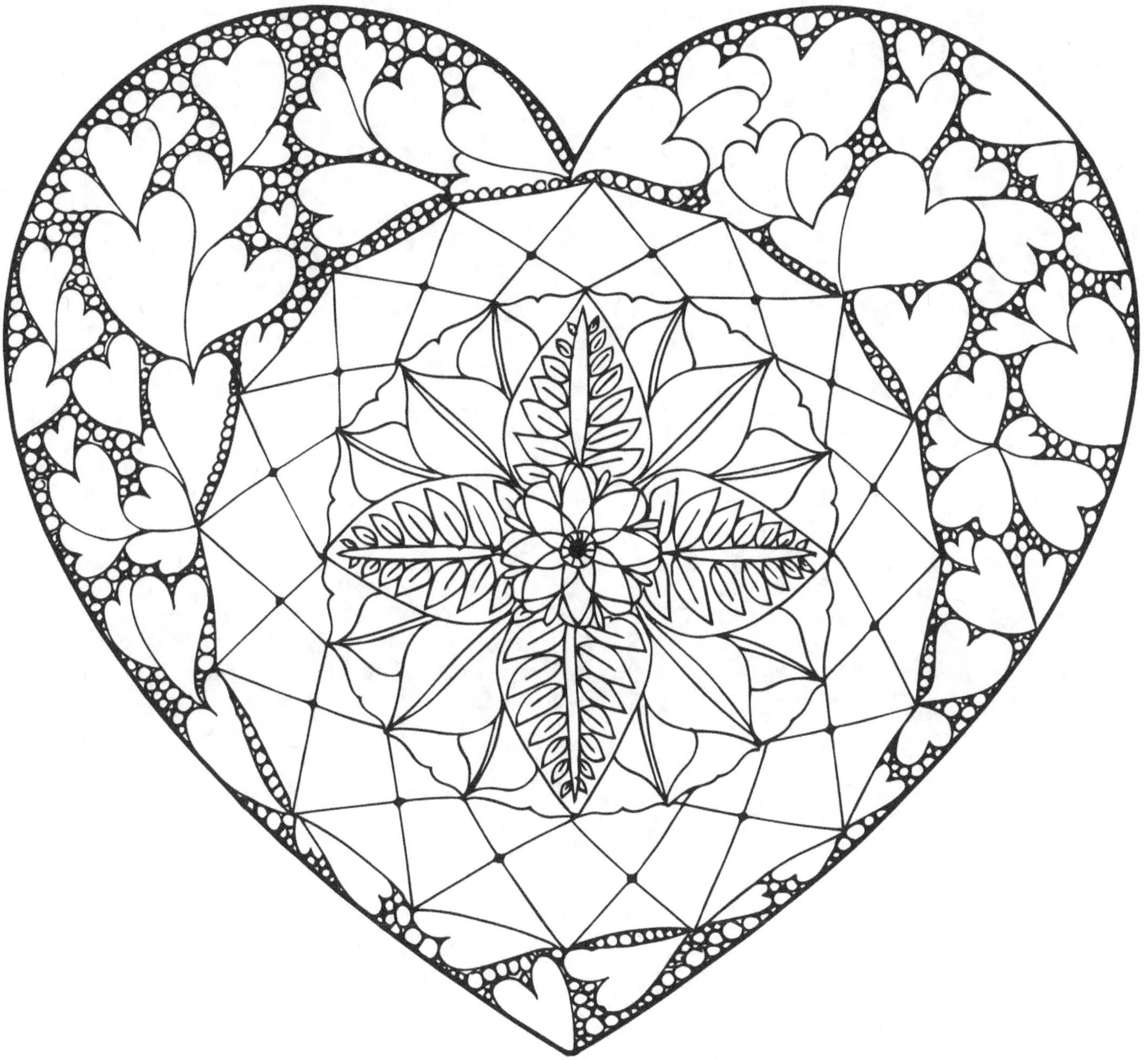

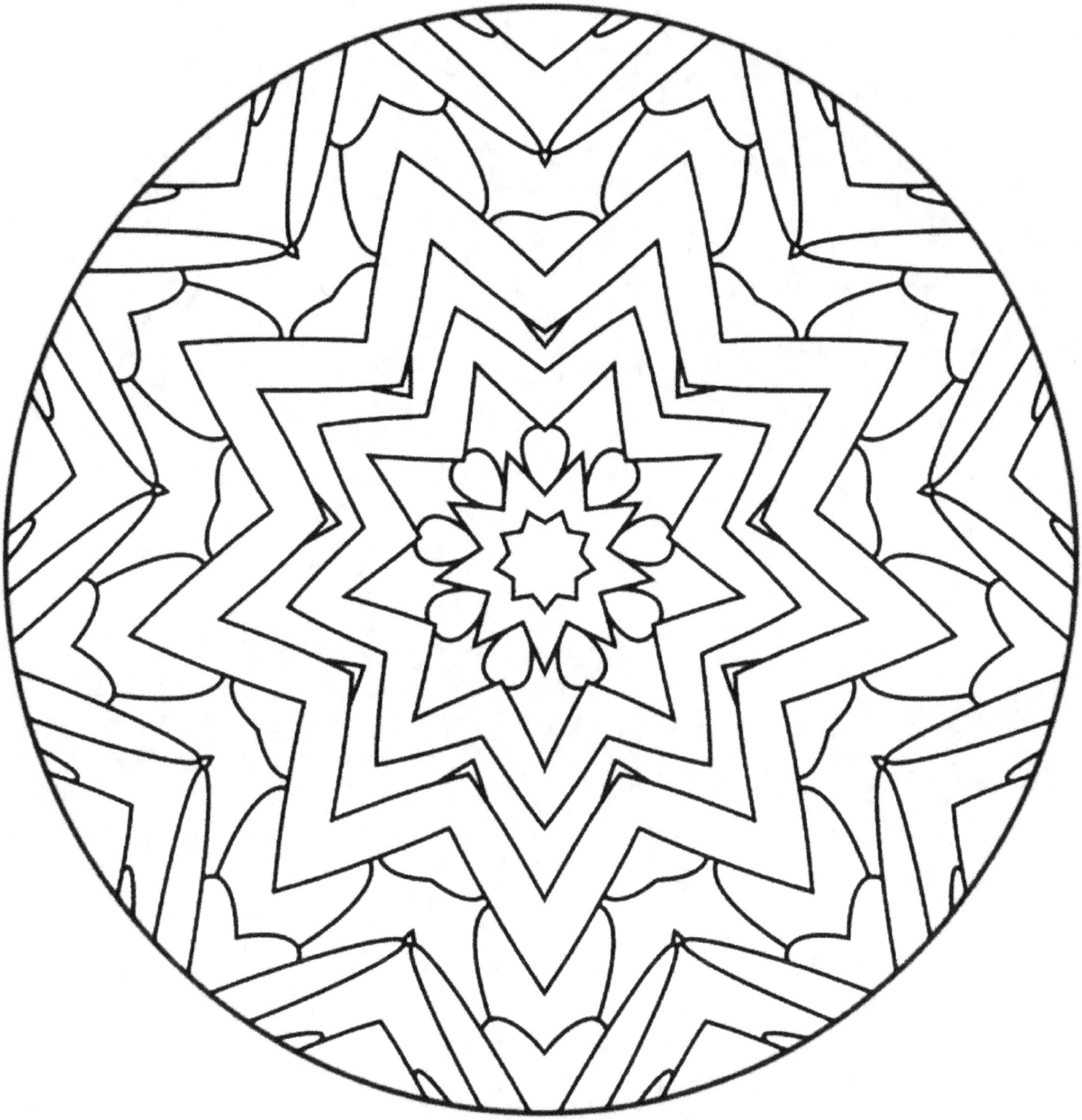

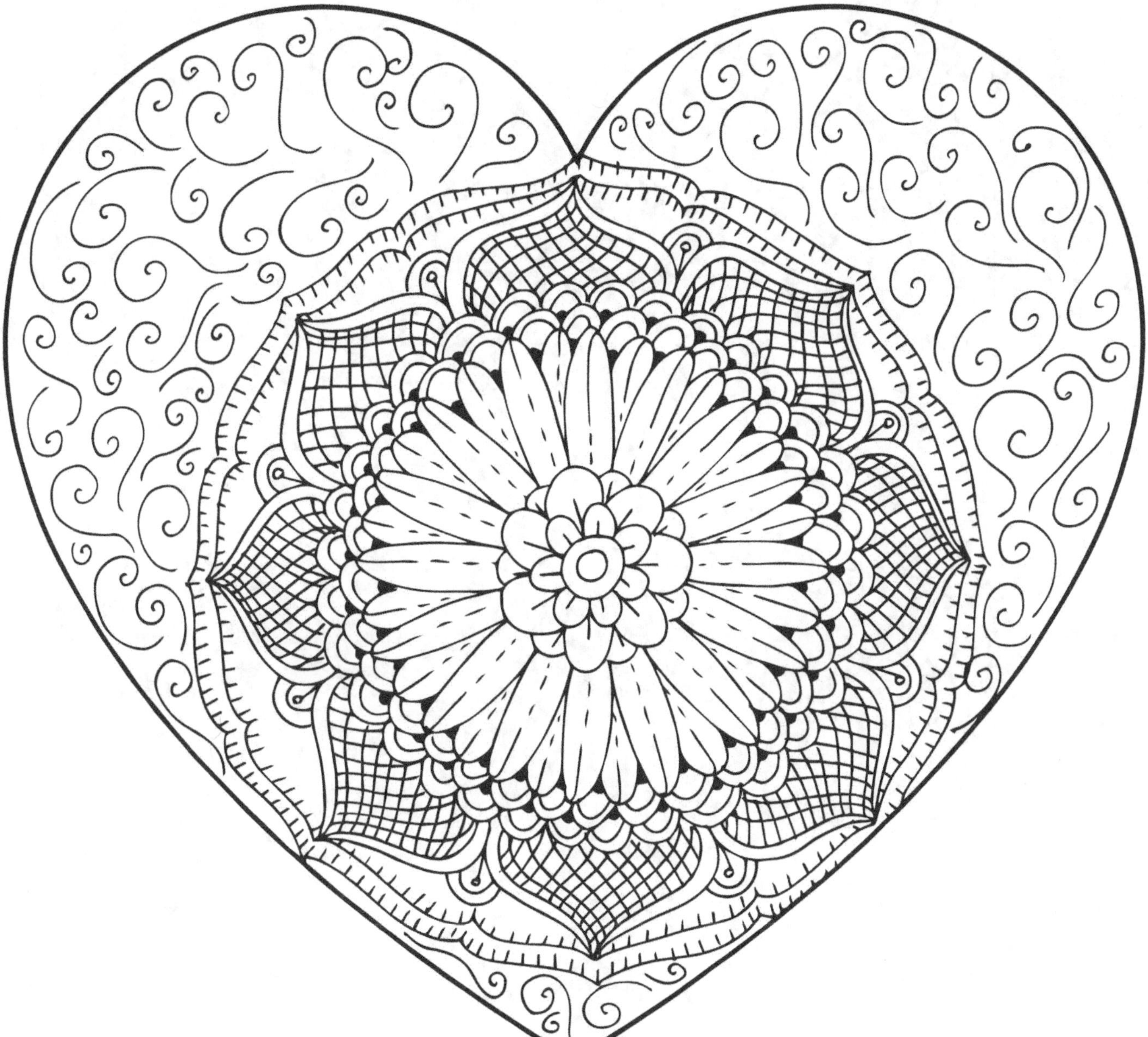

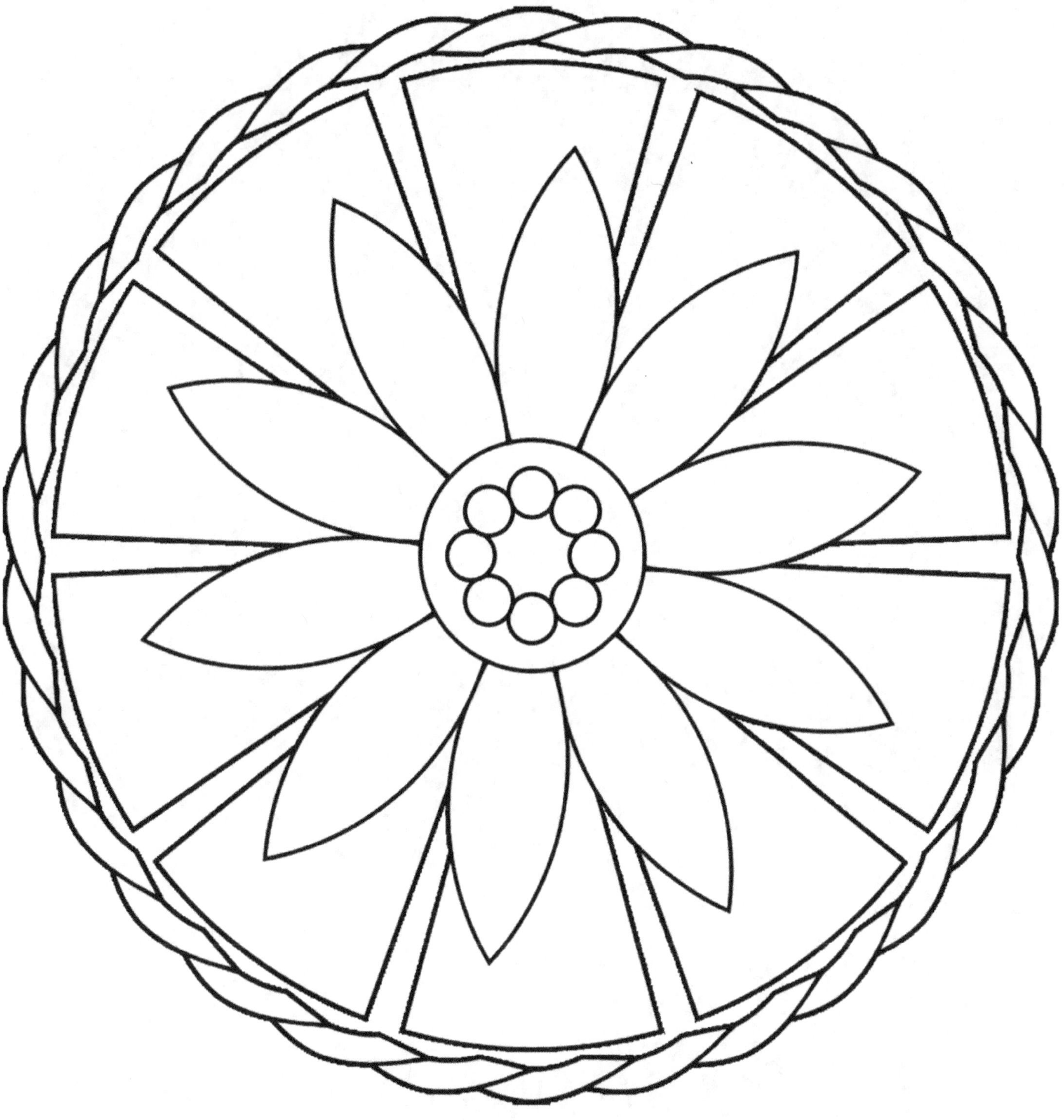

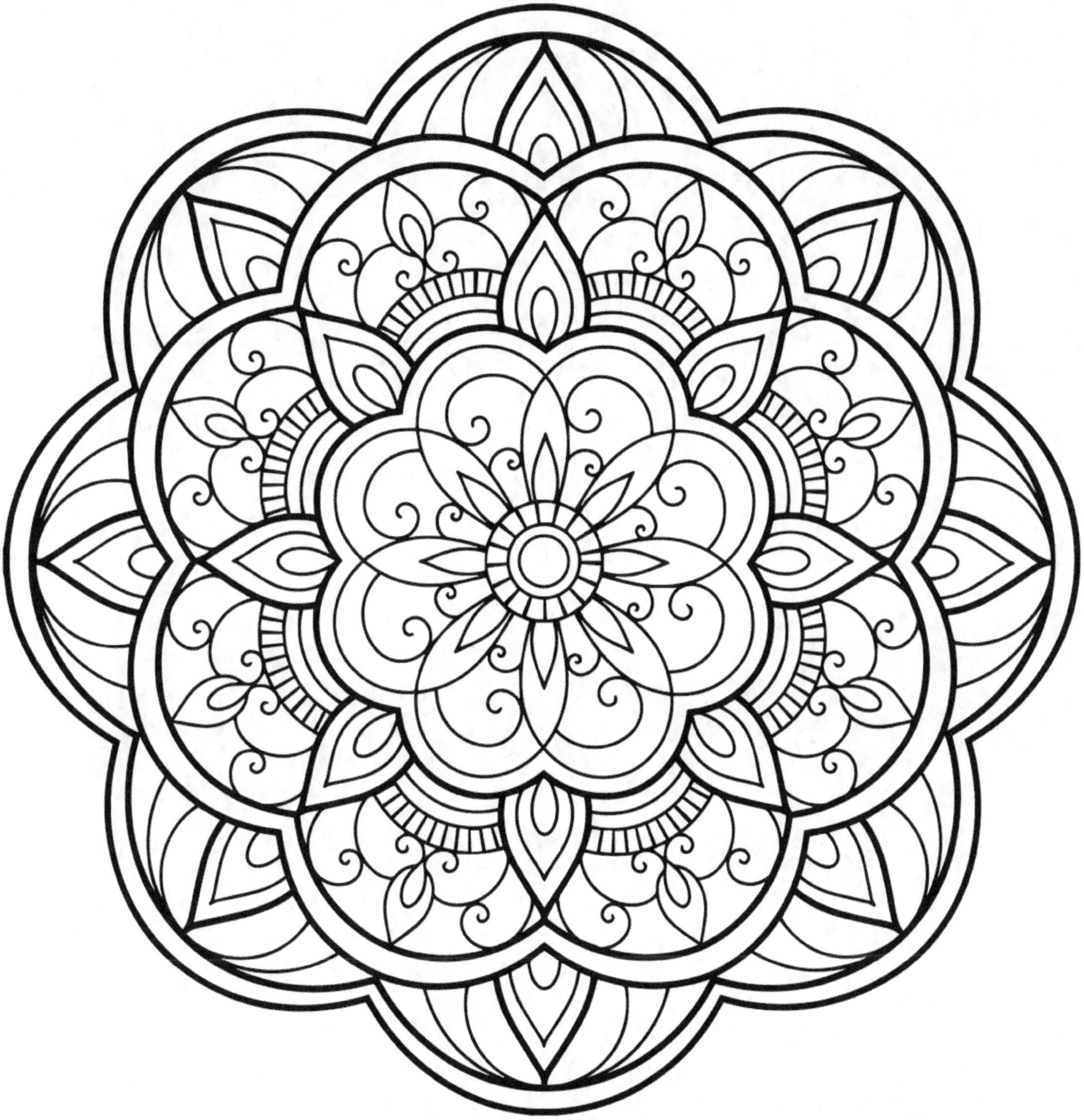

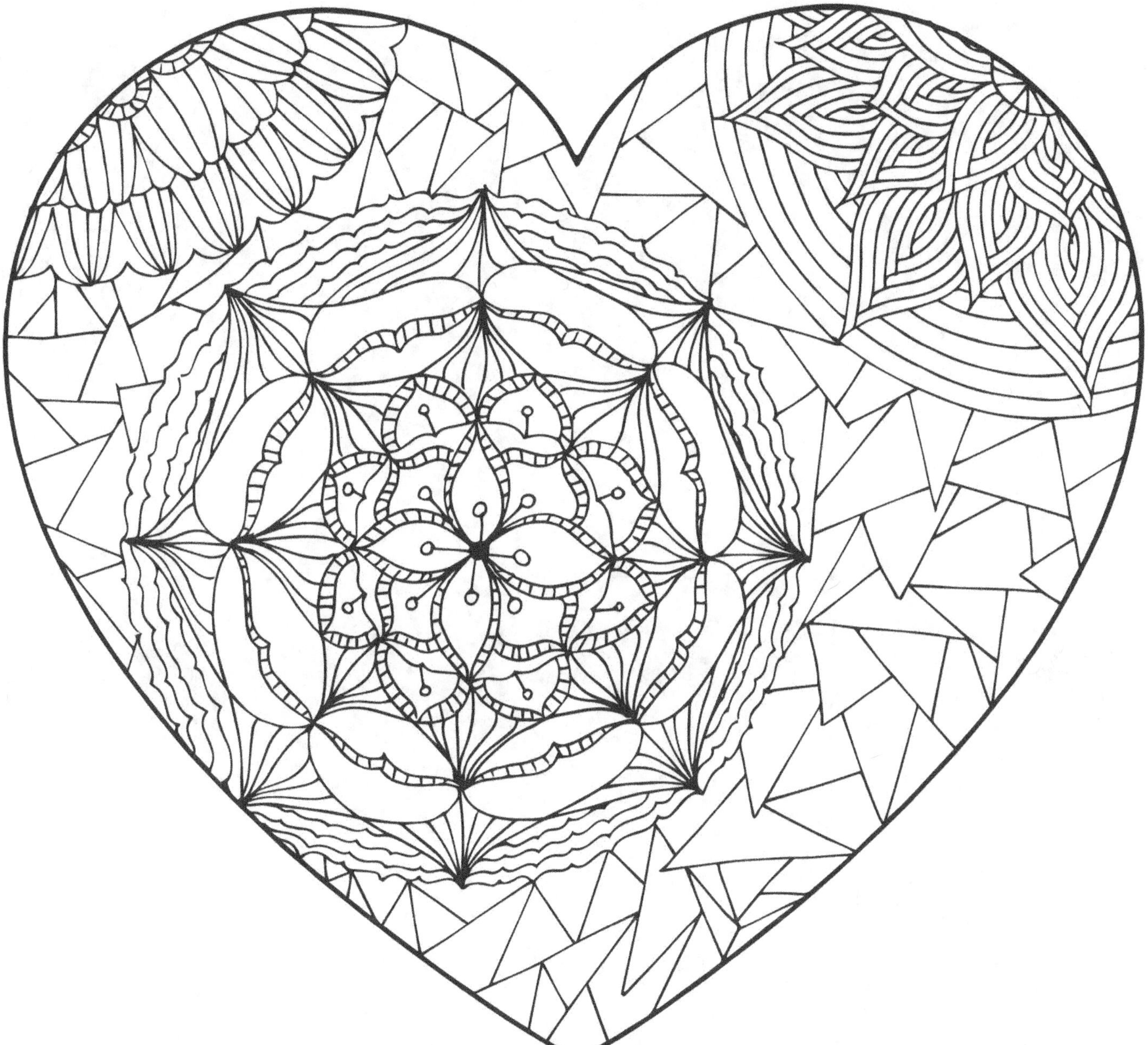

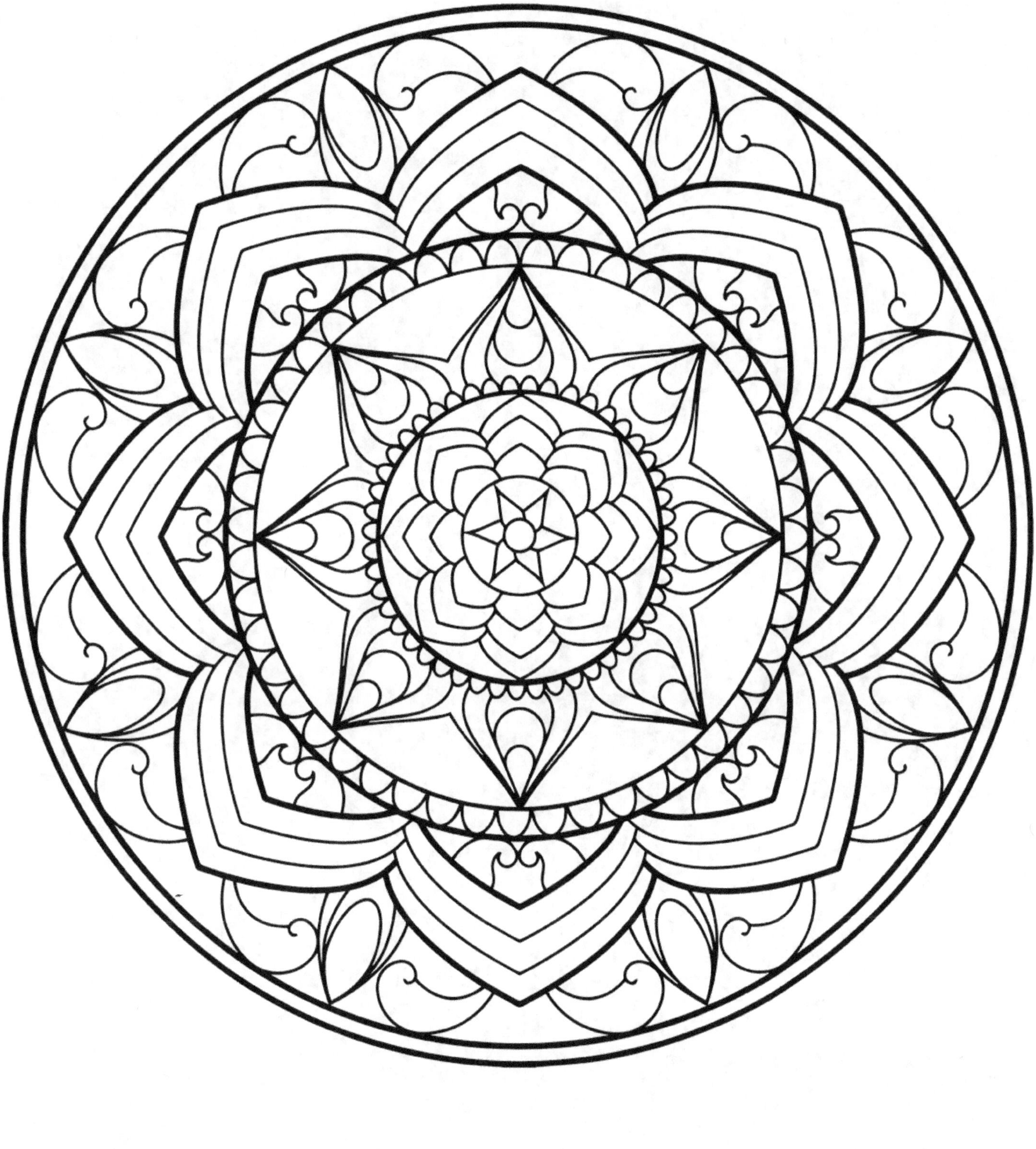

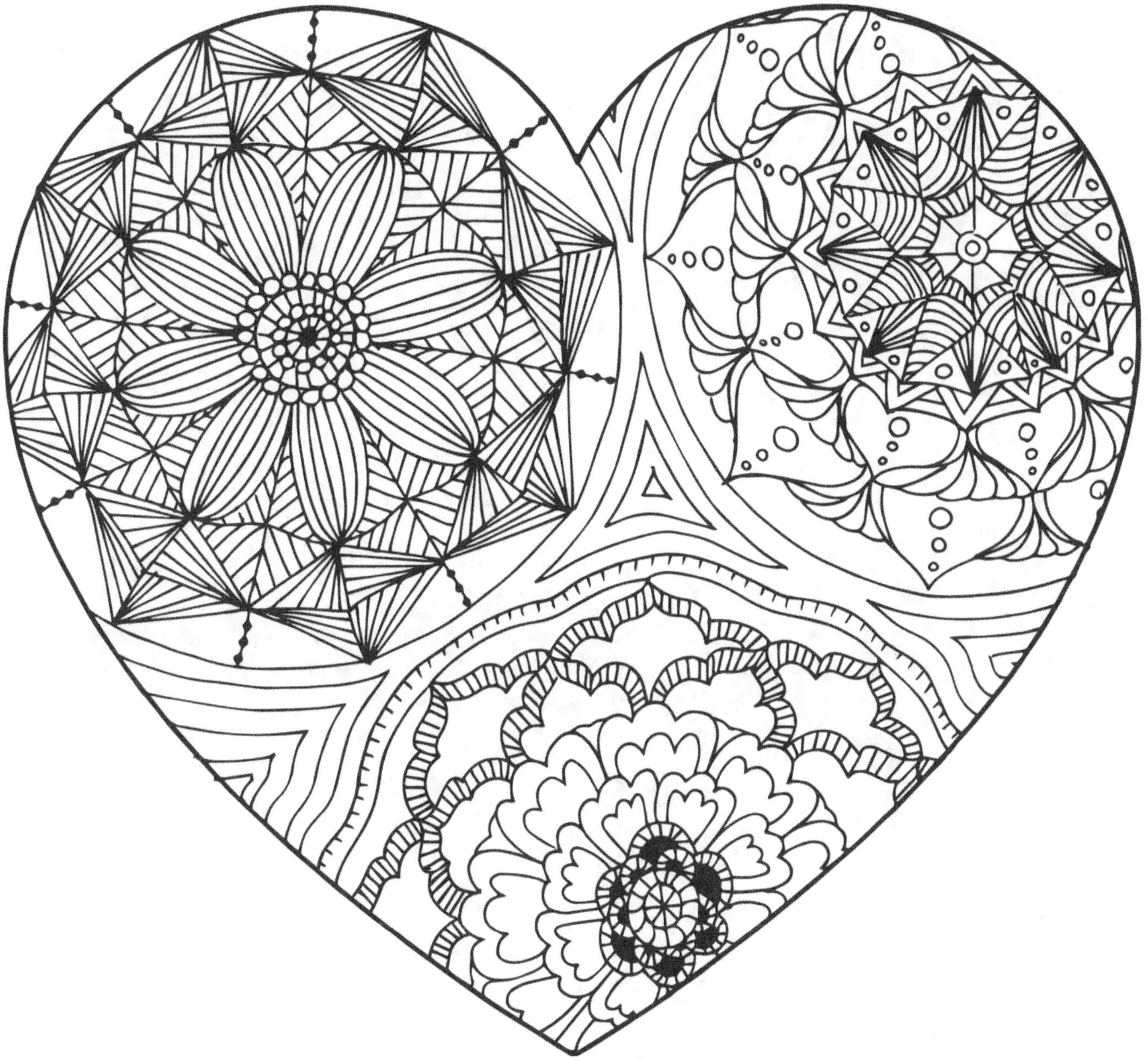

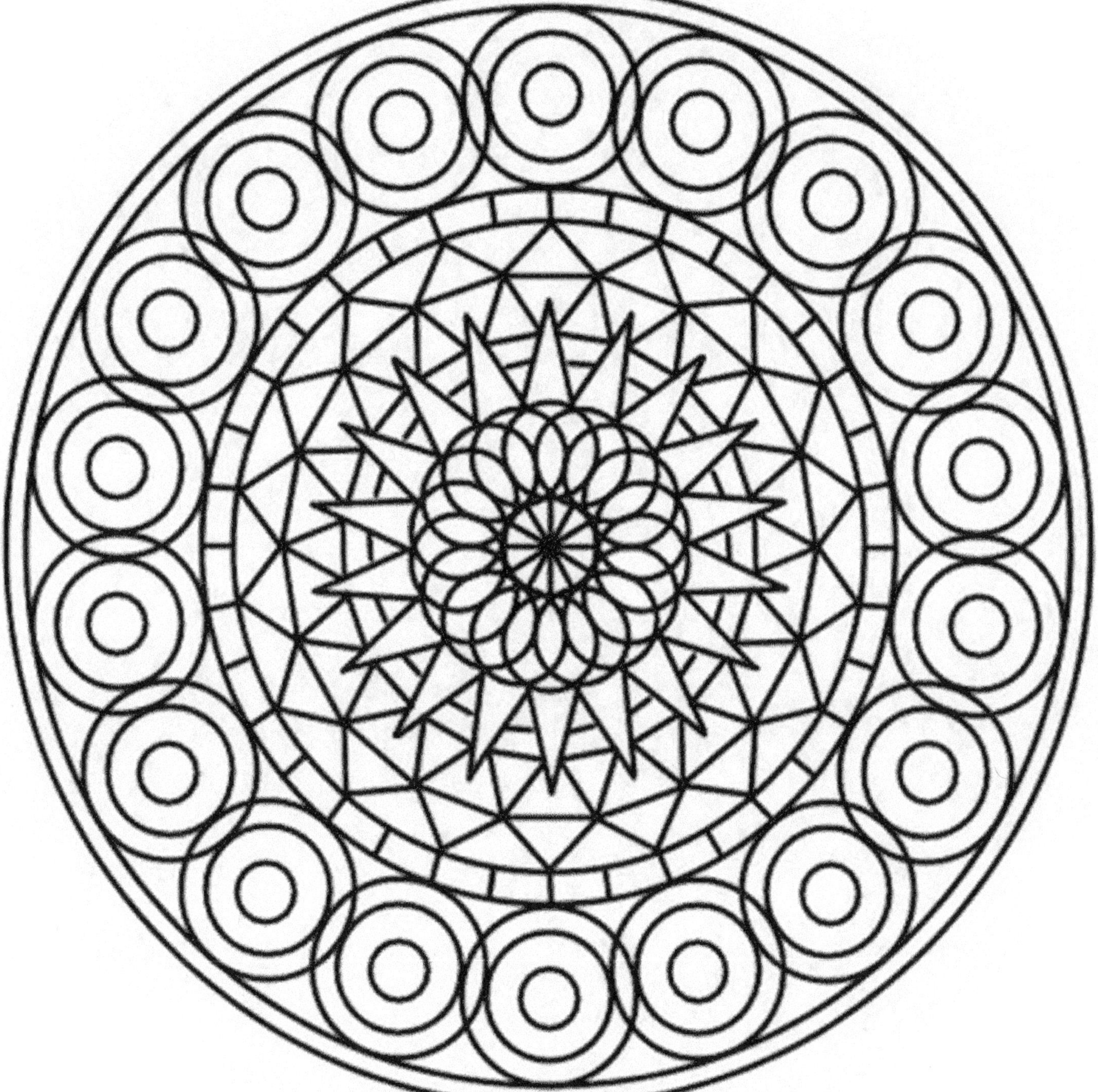

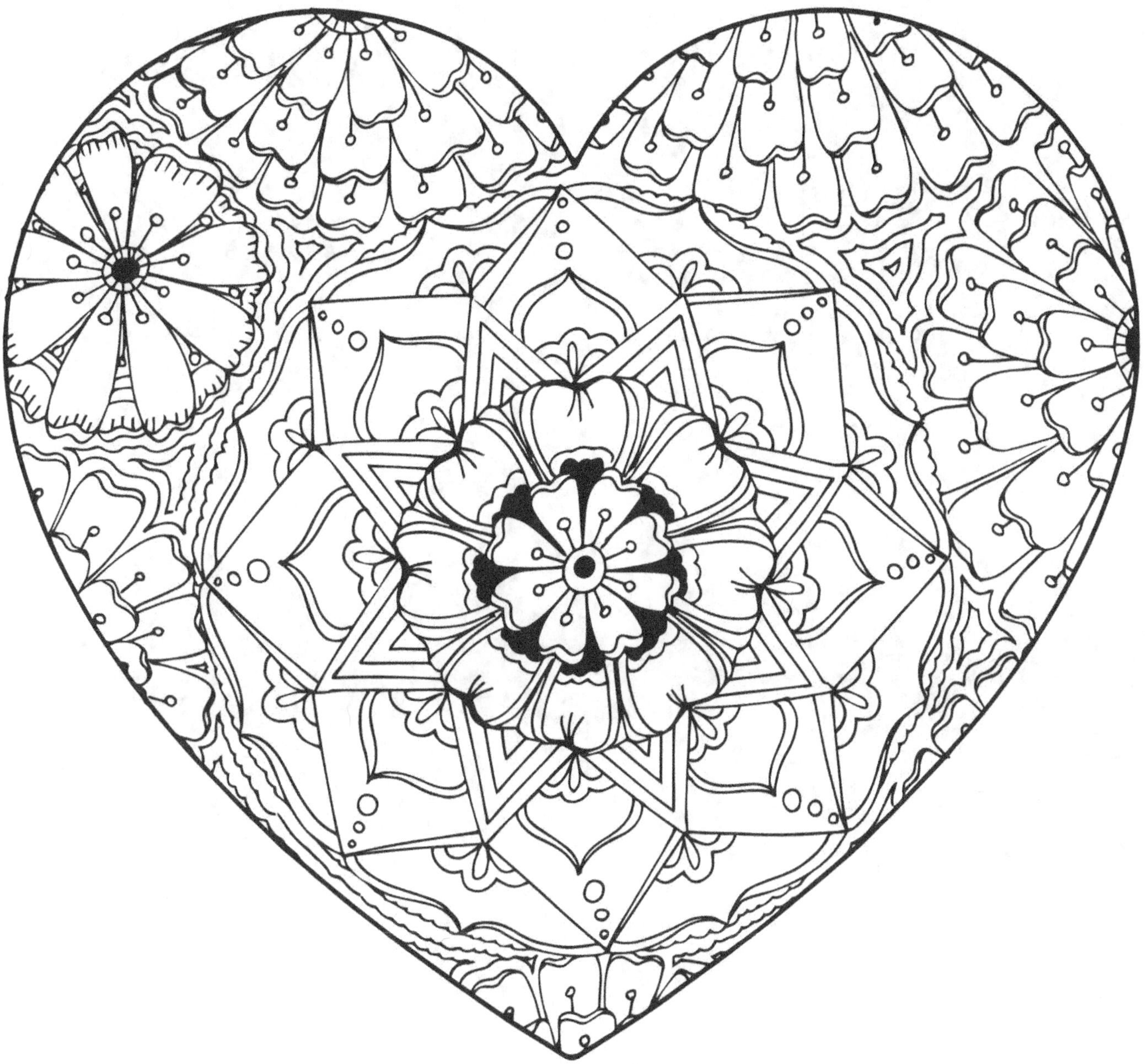

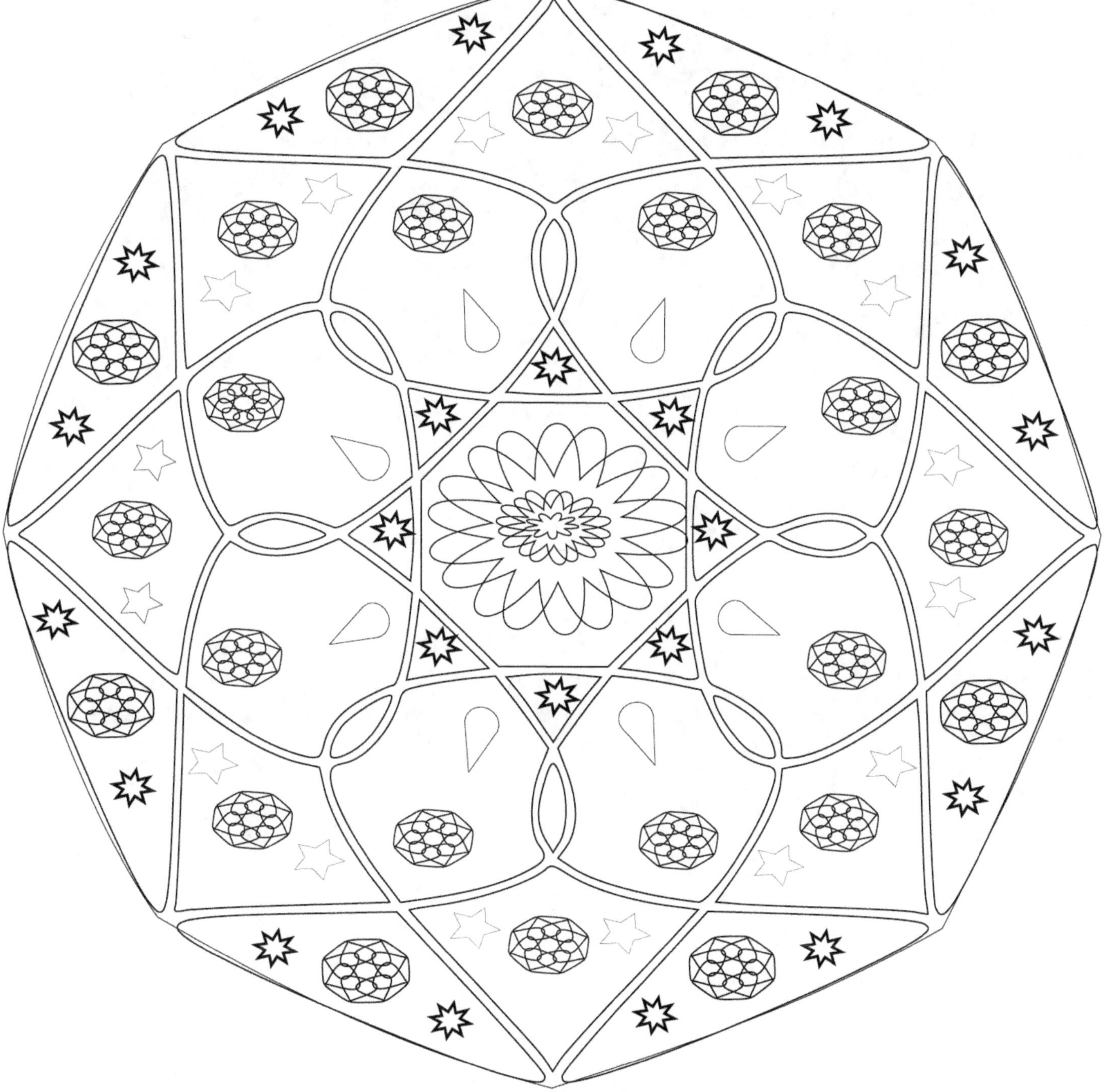

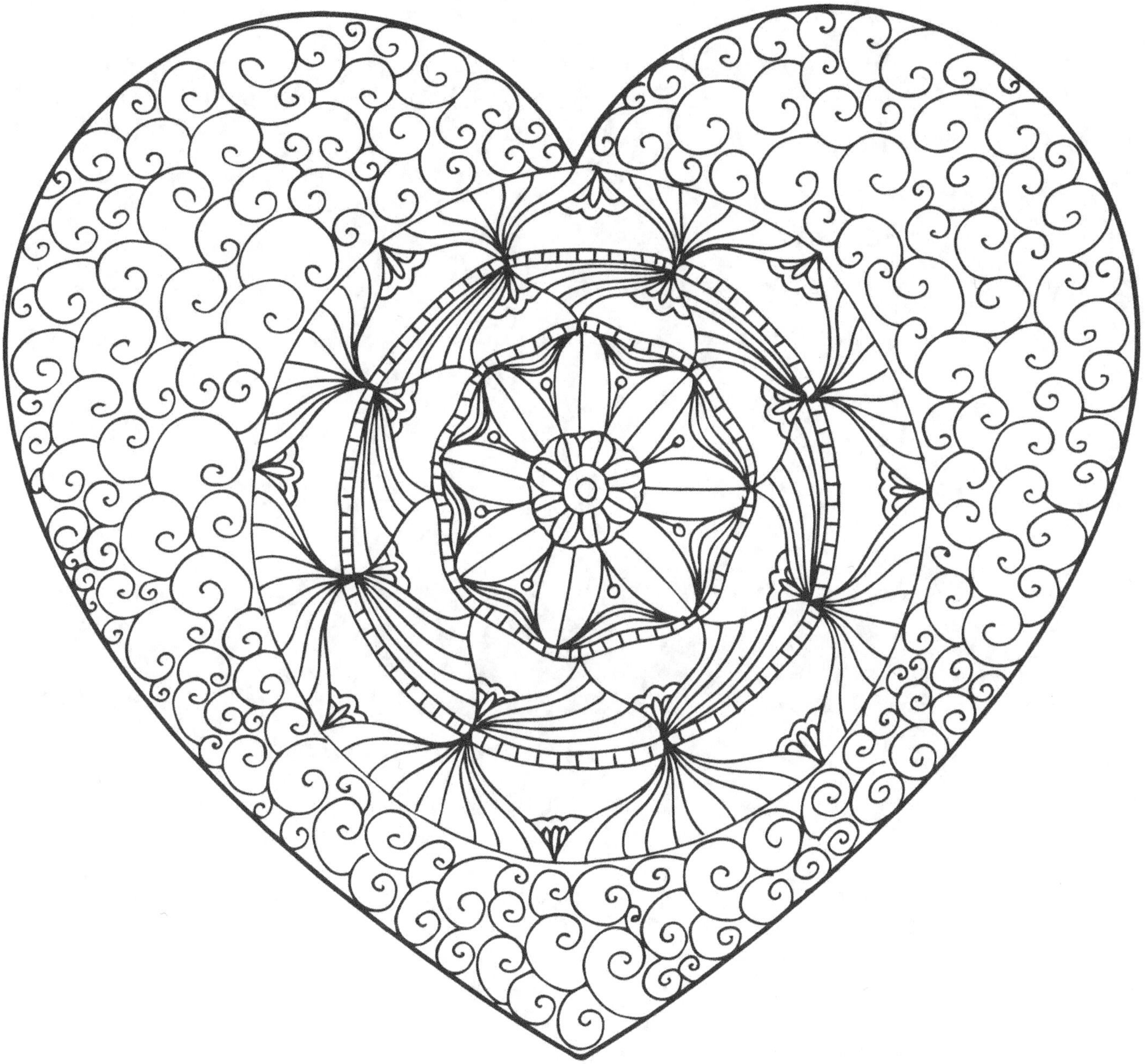

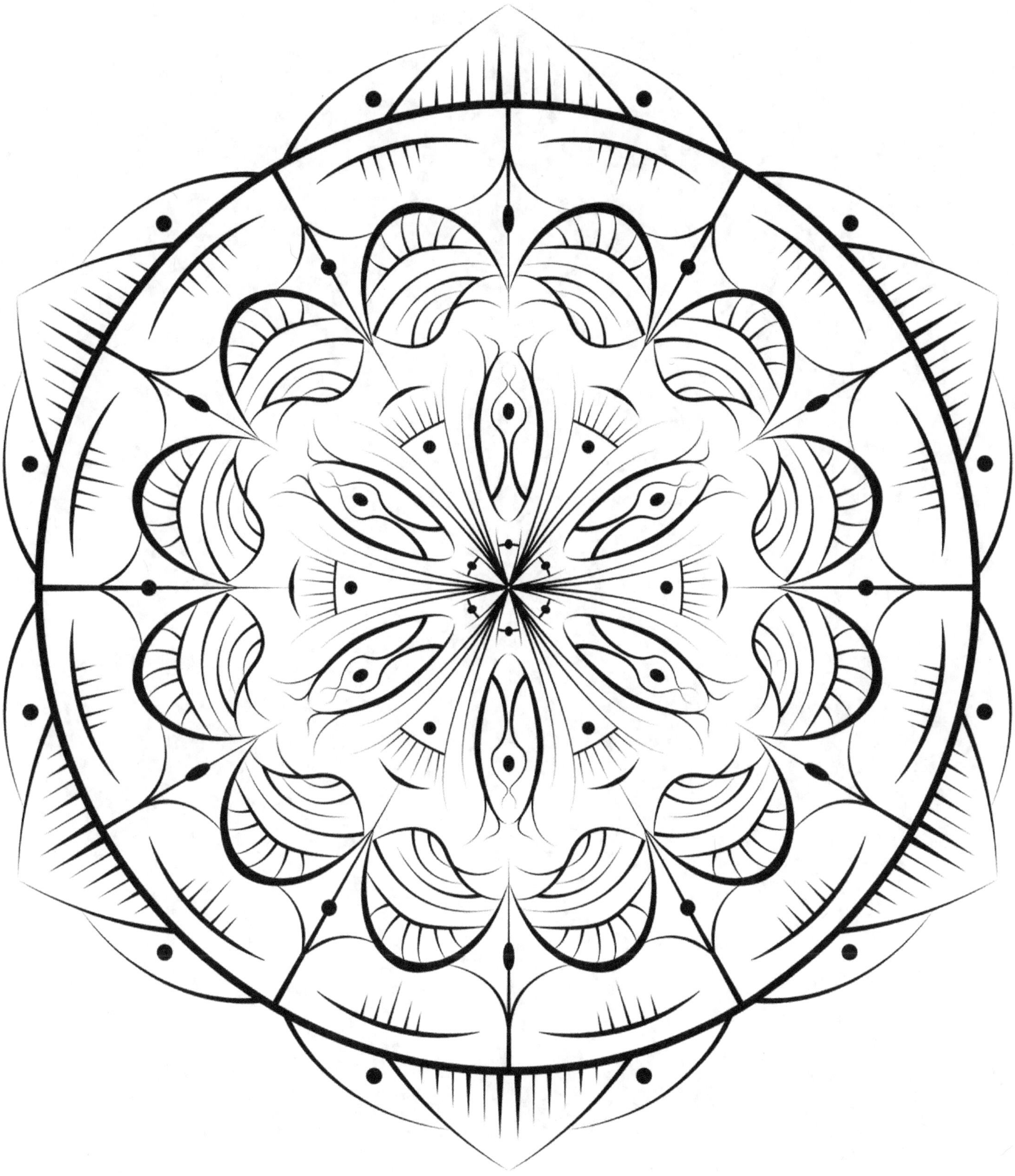

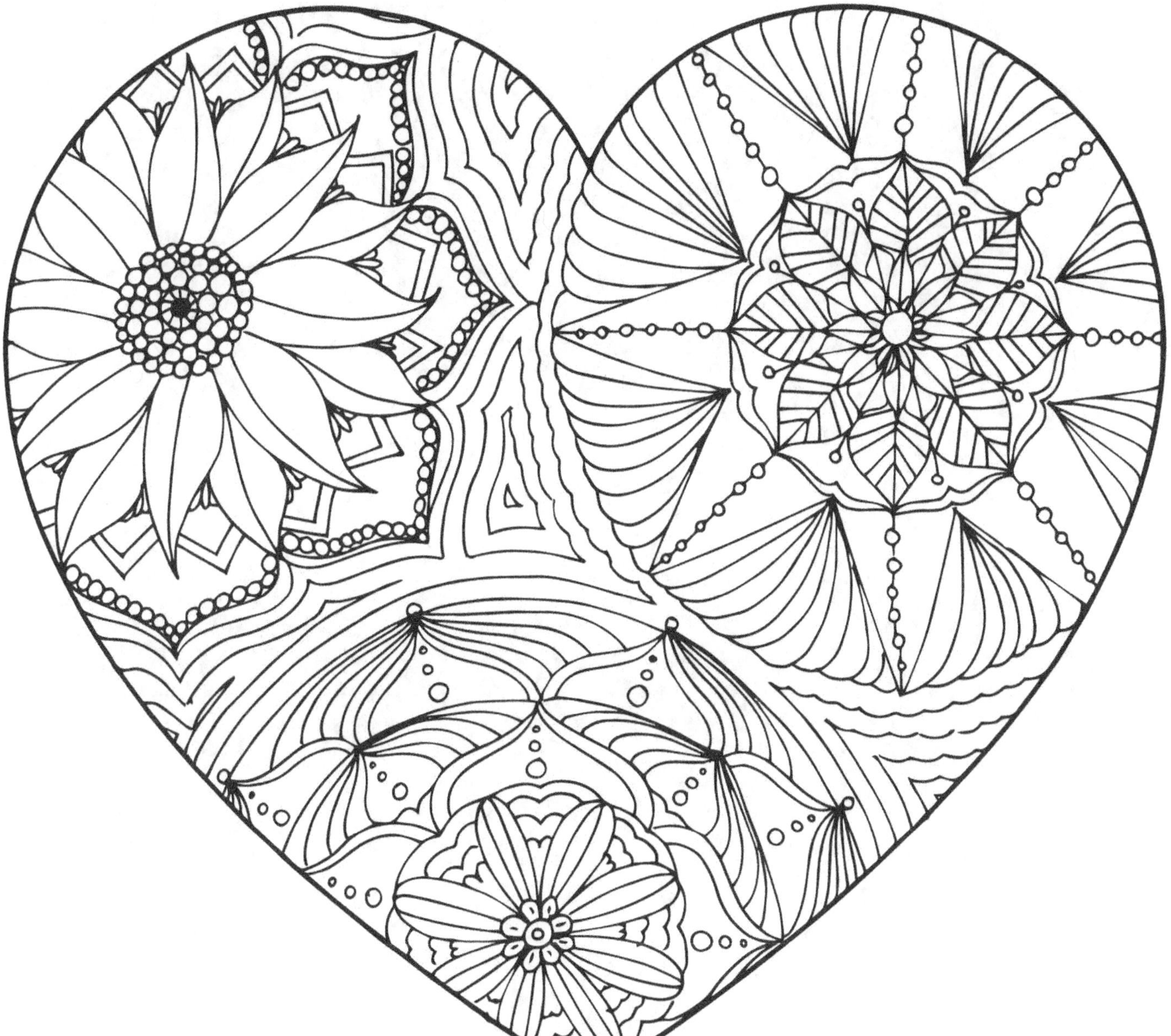

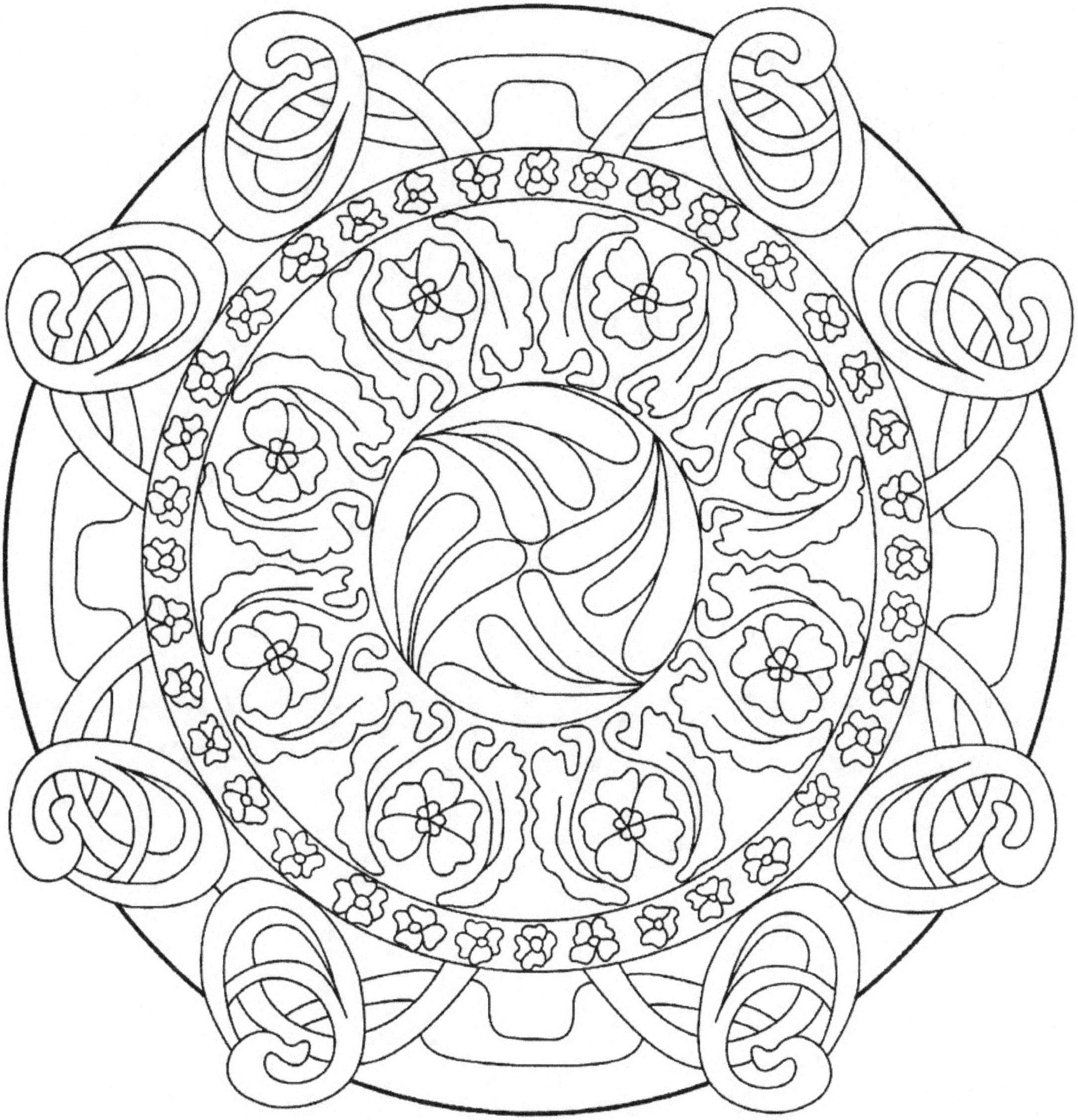

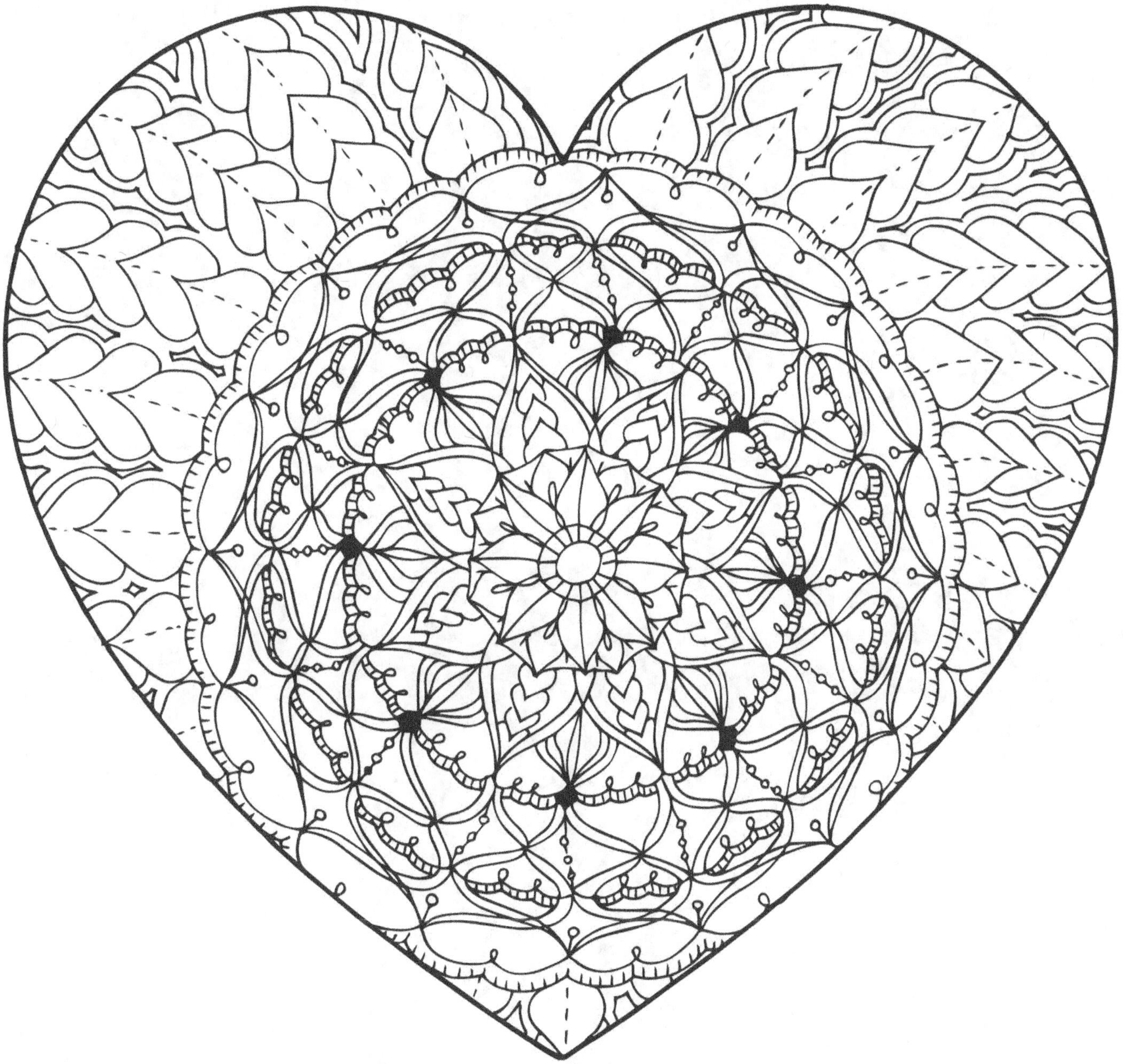

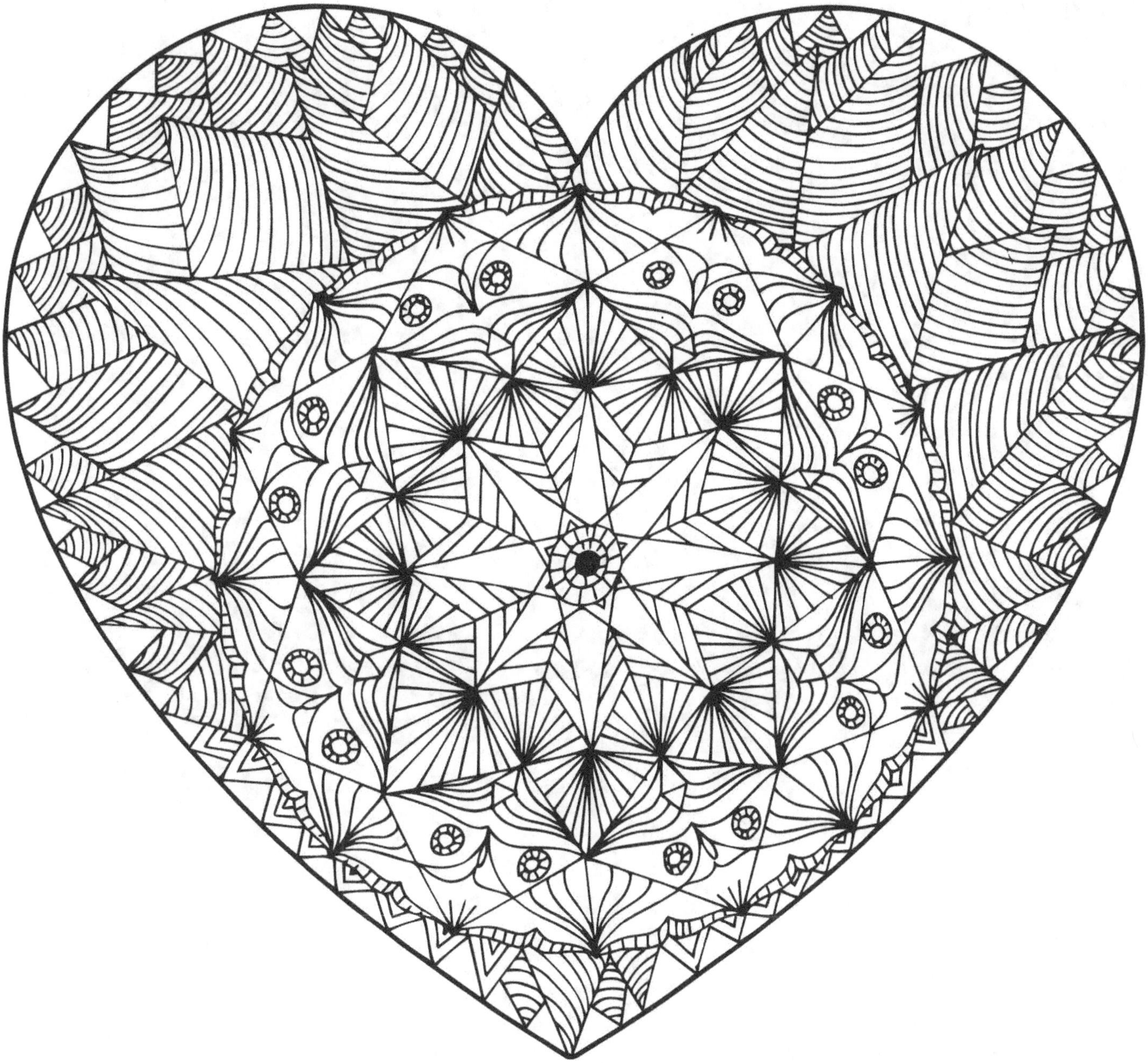

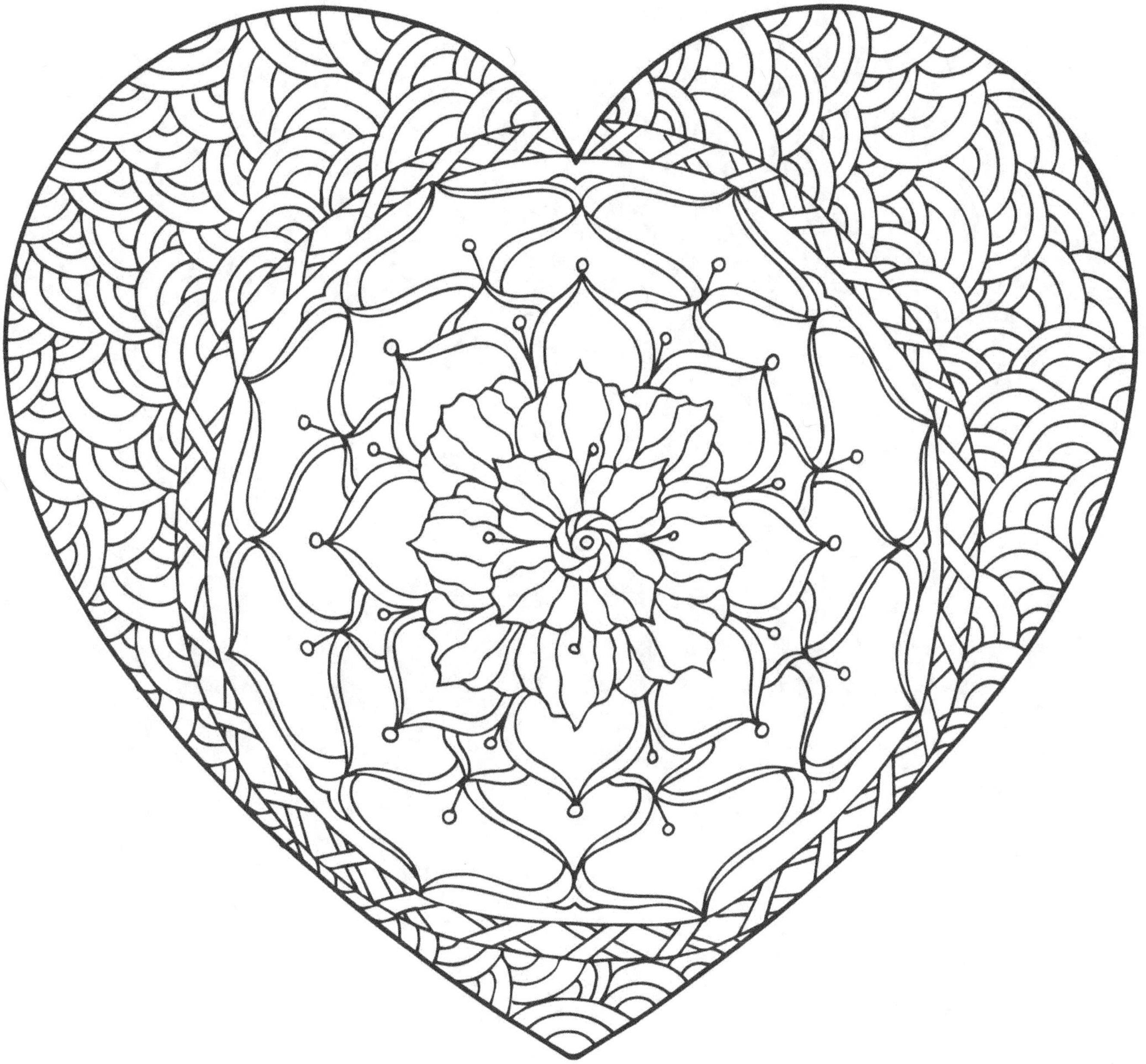

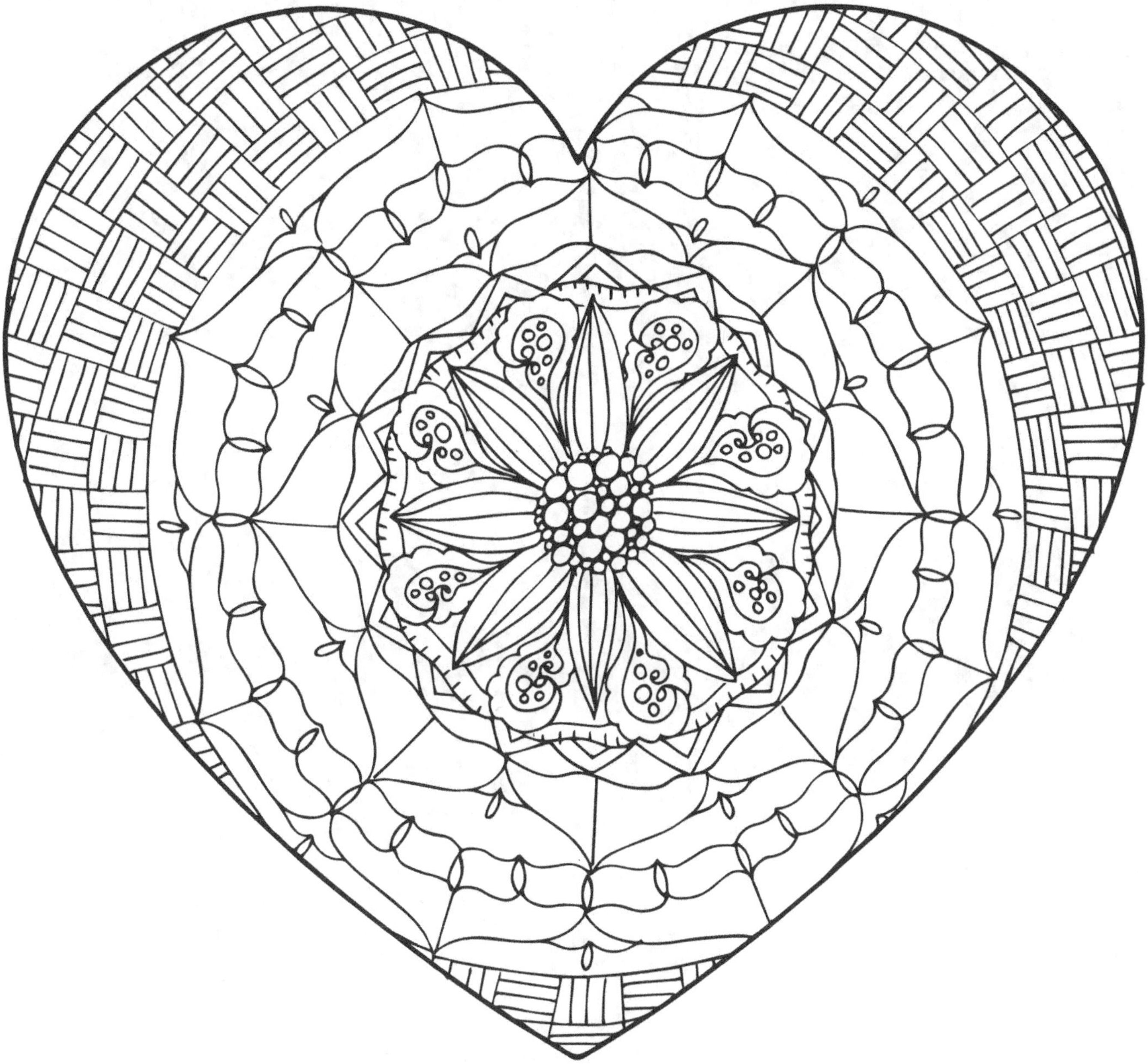

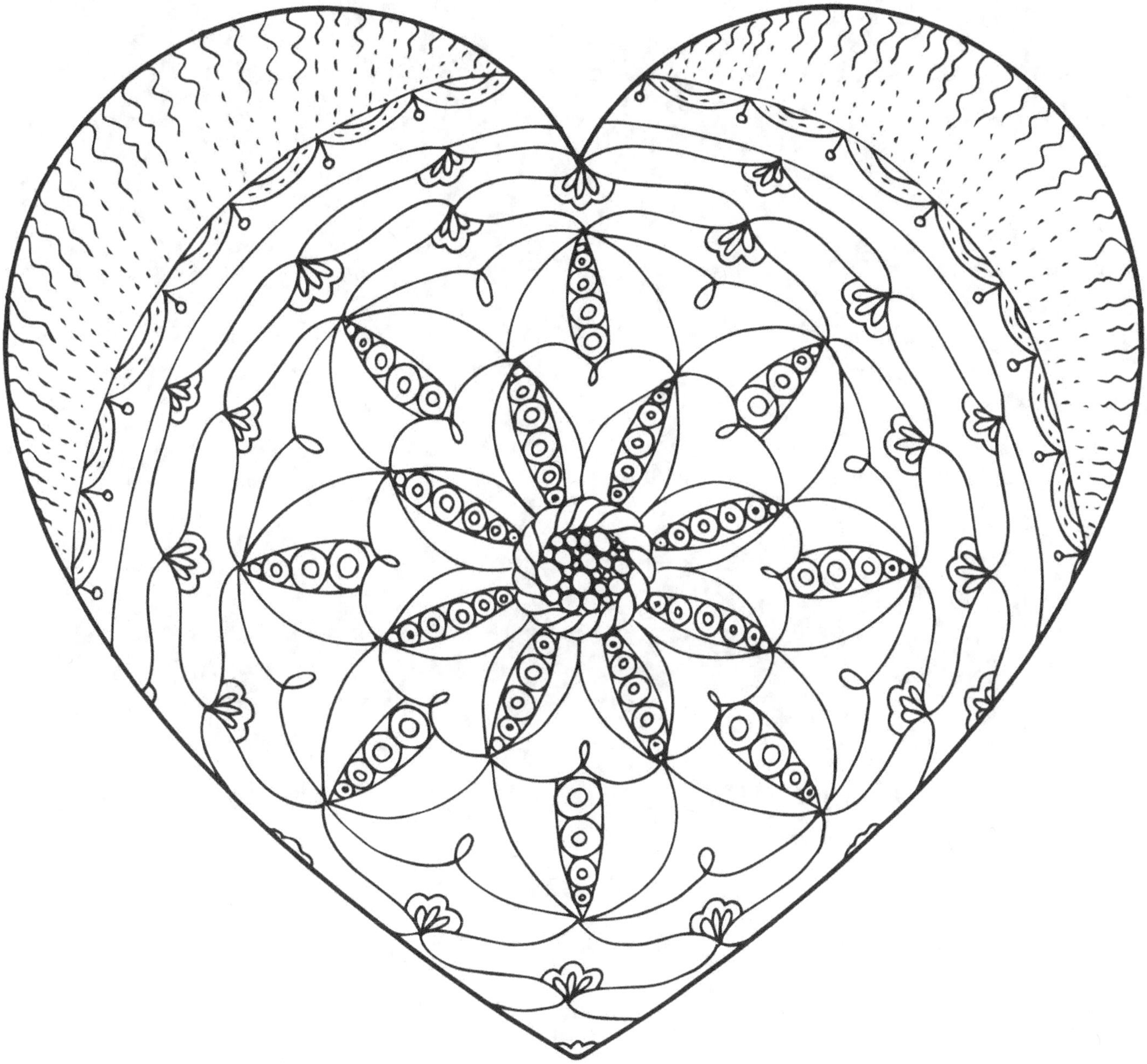

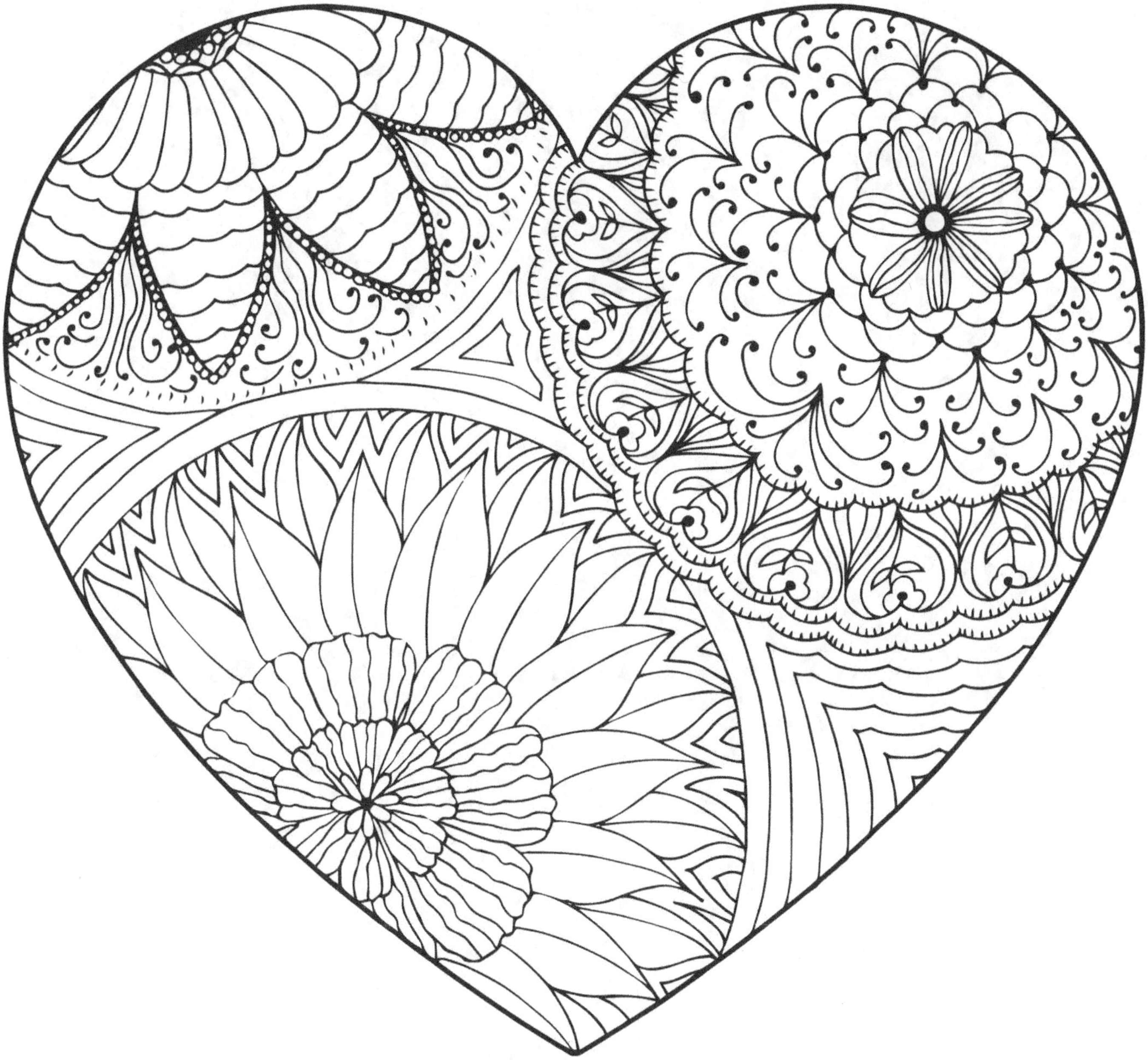

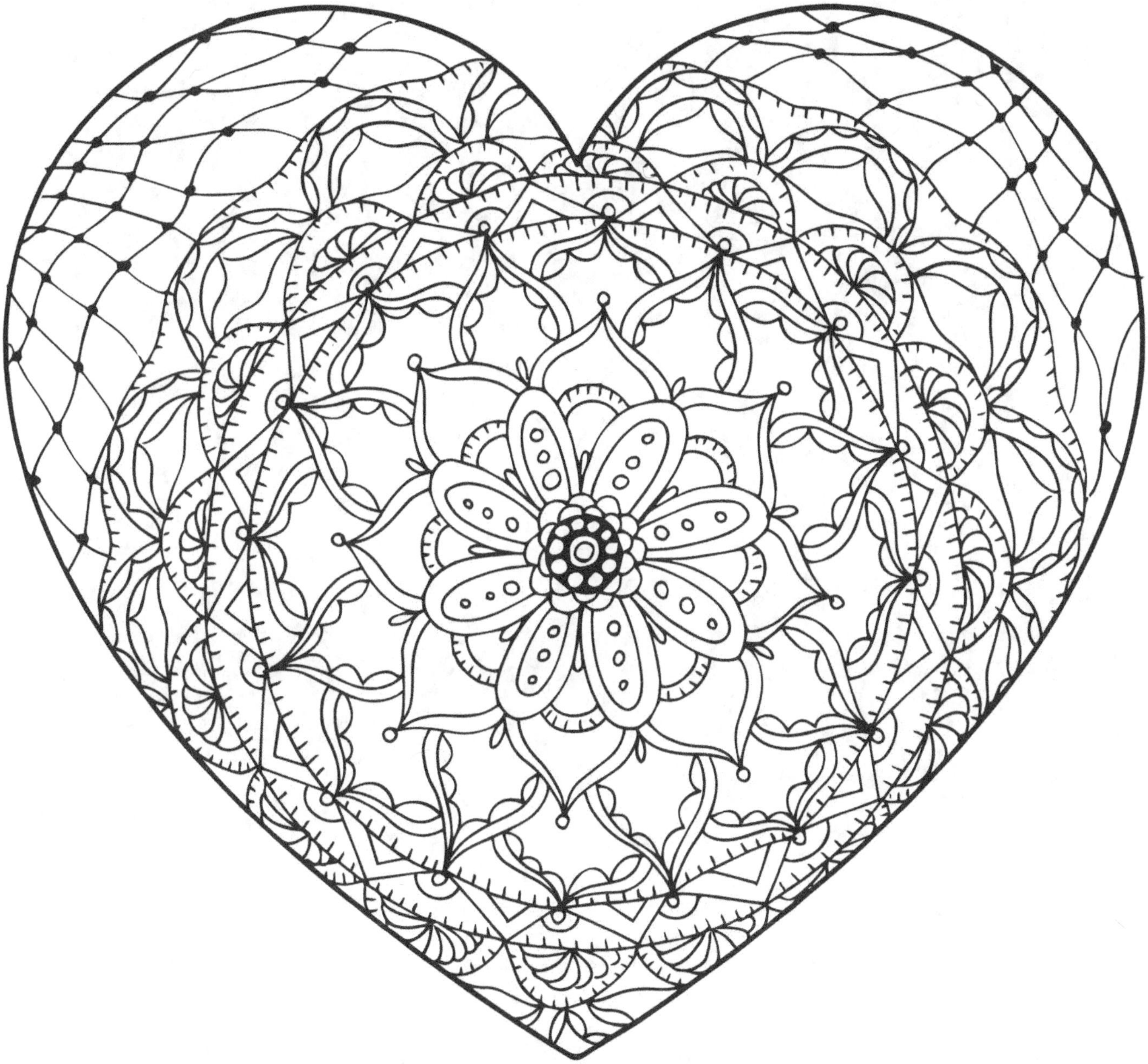

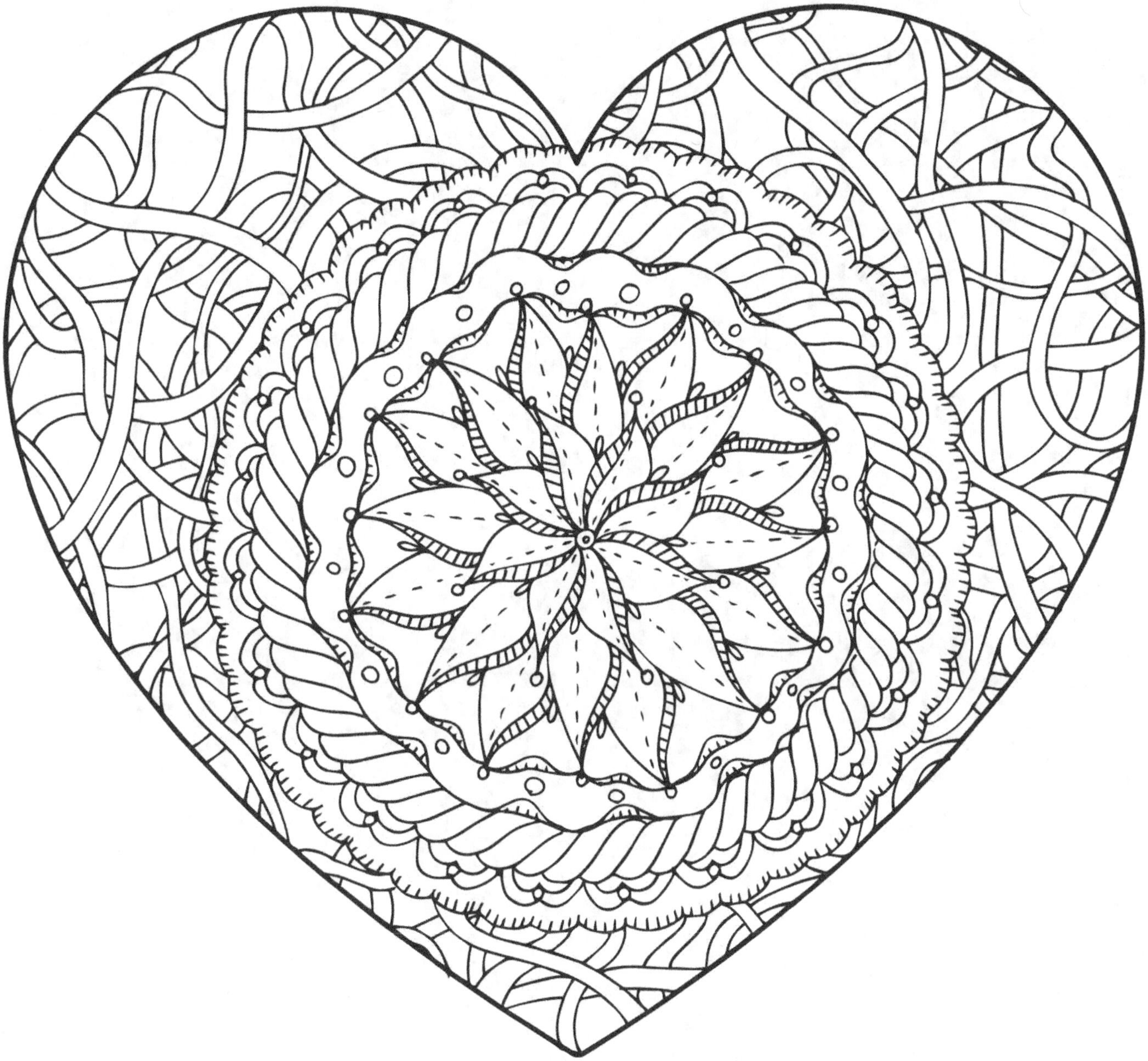

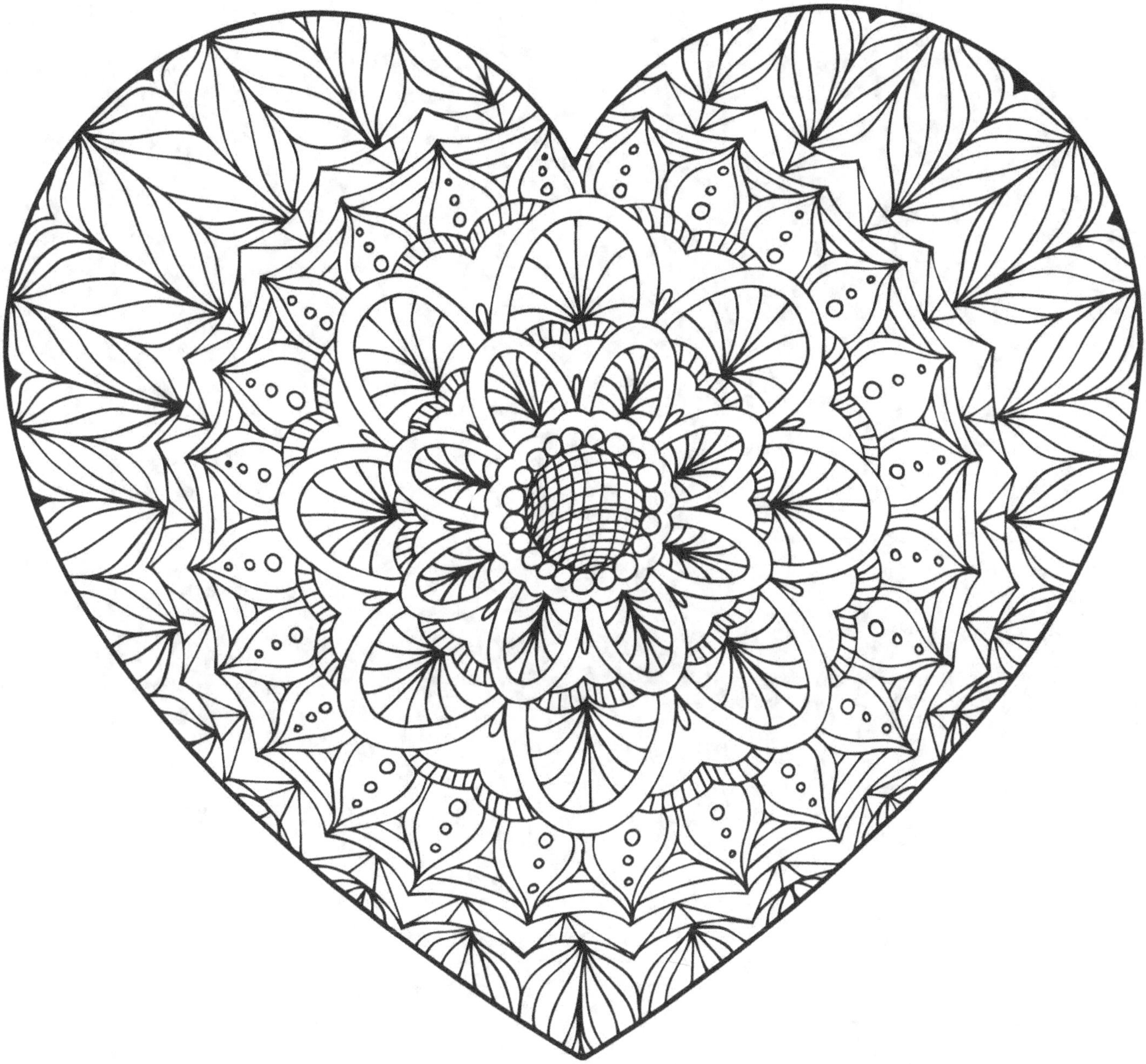

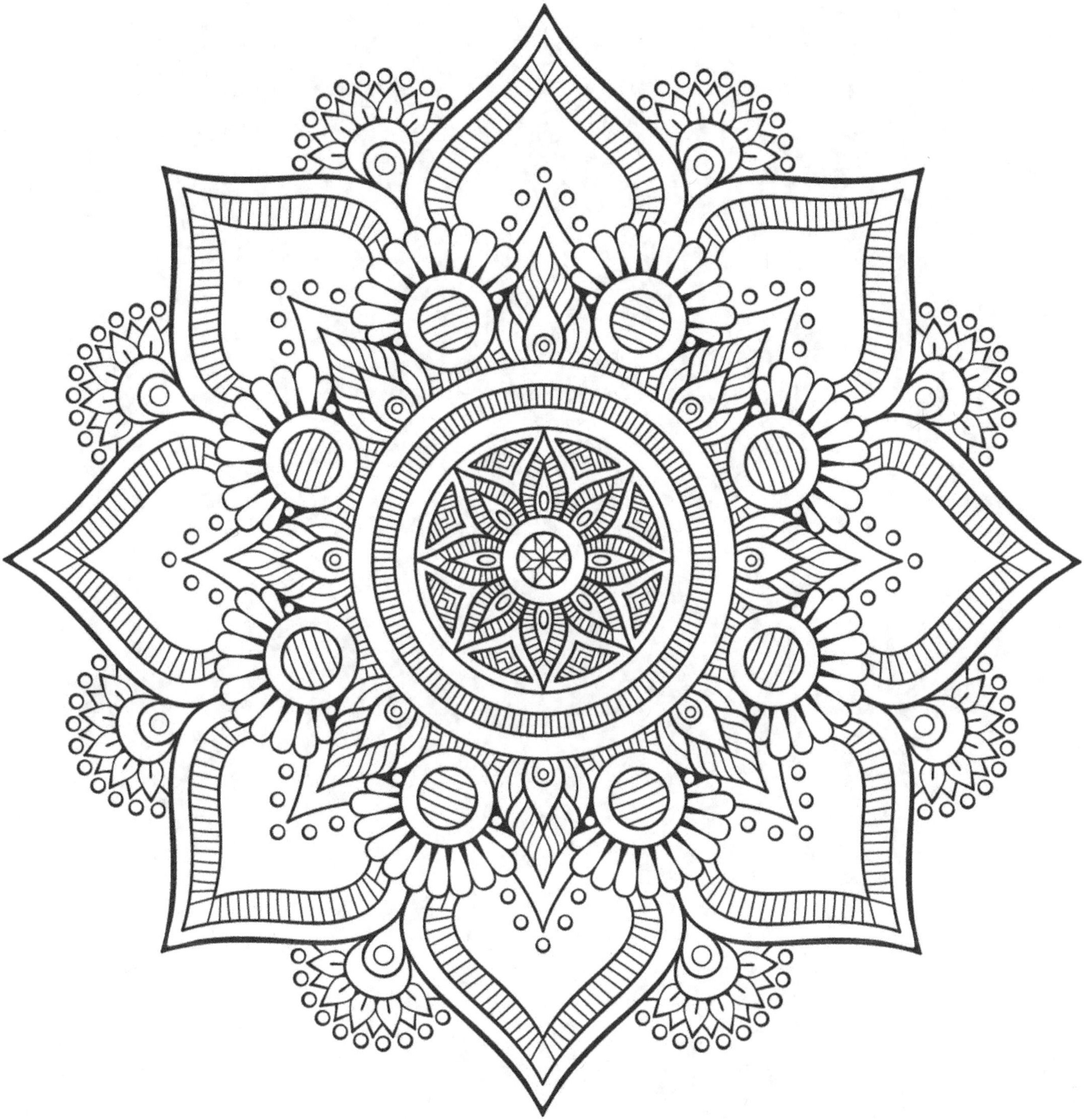

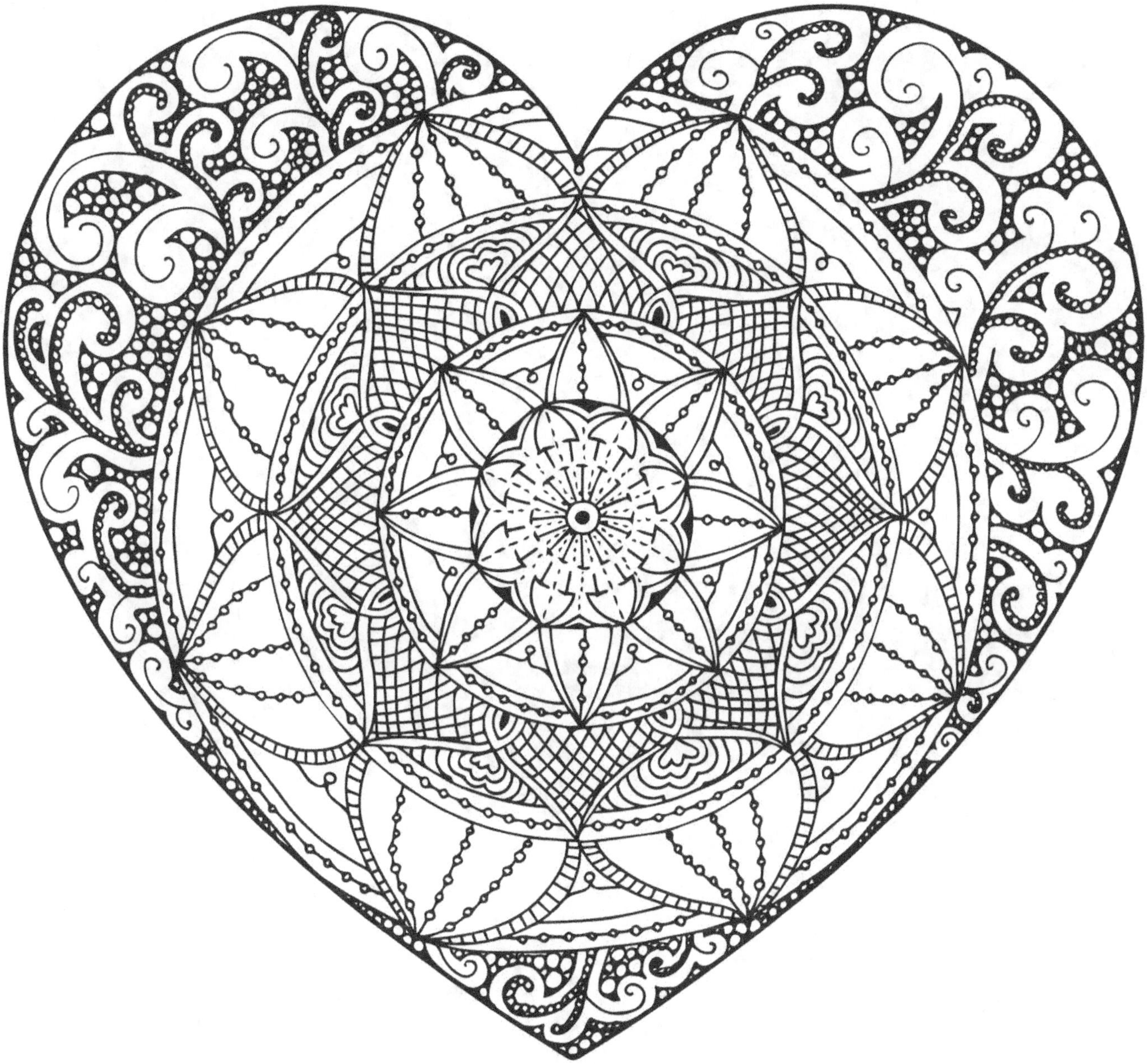

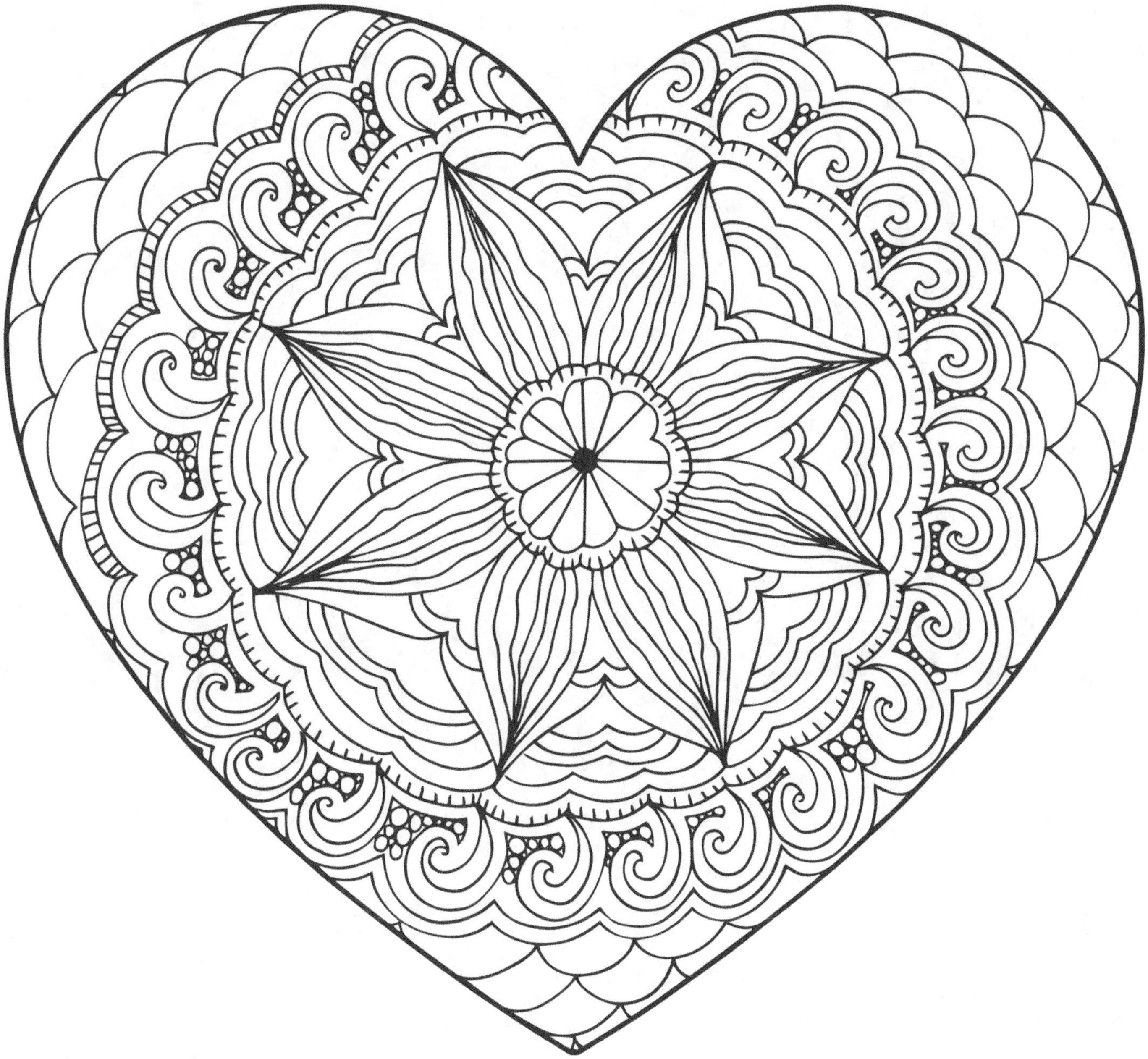

www.ingramcontent.com/pod-product-compliance
Lightning Source LLC
Chambersburg PA
CBHW081446220526
45466CB00008B/2525
9781675769898